FLYING HIGH

MOROCCO

FLYING HIGH

WHITES ART PUBLISHERS

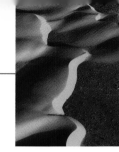

FLYING HIGH MOROCCO

PHOTOGRAPHS

Antonio Attini

Text
PAOLO GALLIANI

Editorial Coordination
MARCELLO LIBRA
ALBERTO BERTOLAZZI

Graphic Design
PAOLA PIACCO

Cover
The fortified village of Ait Benhaddou lies on a
rise along the so-called Valley of Marvels.

Back cover
This open area lined with the Hassan Tower,
the Mohammed V Mausoleum and the
mosque is the religious and monumental
heart of Rabat.

1
A number of vacation resorts have grown up by
the turquoise sea at Ksar Sghir.

2-3
Contrasts in the High Atlas: vegetation and cultivated
fields face to face with the first strips of the desert.

4-5
The bastions of Essaouira crown the *medina*.

Contents

6-7 and 8
The Sahara around Laayoune is inhospitable and awesome, and may disturb those who do not like silence and wide-open spaces.

9
The Mausoleum of Hassan is one of the landmarks in Rabat.

10
The Draa River valley is a strip of green in the middle of the desert.

11
Lagoons and fountains between the desert and the ocean. Curious salt lake depressions often develop around Tarfaya.

12-13
The highest peaks are grouped together in the massif between the provinces of Marrakech and Ouarzazate, dominated by Mt Toukal (13,671 ft/4167 m).

14-15
Almost overrun with palm and olive trees, Tamelelt is a labyrinth of streets and low houses at the edge of the desert.

16-17
Flotsam on the beautiful ocean beach of Tarfaya.

The
author

ANTONIO ATTINI, WAS BORN IN TURIN IN 1960 AND HAS PRODUCED NUMEROUS PHOTO REPORTS IN EUROPE, AFRICA, ASIA AND AMERICA, WHICH HAVE BEEN PUBLISHED BY THE WORLD'S LEADING TRAVEL MAGAZINES. HE HAS WORKED WITH WHITE STAR PUBLISHERS SINCE 1989, TAKING THE PHOTOGRAPHS FOR NUMEROUS VOLUMES IN THE "COUNTRIES OF THE WORLD", "ALL AMERICA" AND "PLACES AND HISTORY" SERIES, AND CONTRIBUTING TO THE CREATION OF MANY OTHER PRESTIGIOUS WORKS. ATTINI HAS BEEN A MEMBER OF THE KODAK GOLD CIRCLE SINCE 1994, WITH THE STANDARD OF EXCELLENCE. IN RECENT YEARS HE HAS SPECIALIZED IN AERIAL PHOTOGRAPHY, SHOOTING FEATURES FROM THE SKIES OF AMERICA AND EUROPE, AND FOR WHITE STAR HE HAS ALSO WORKED ON SEVERAL BOOKS FOR "THE WORLD FROM THE AIR", "A WORLD OF EMOTIONS" AND "FLYING HIGH" SERIES.

FLYING HIGH MOROCCO

Introduction

UPON HIS RETURN FROM A VACATION SPENT BETWEEN TANGIER AND MARRAKECH, JACQUES BREL MADE THE FOLLOWING SUCCINCT COMMENT: "IT IS THE PLACE WHERE ONE CAN FIND EVERYTHING THAT IS LACKING FOR THE PEOPLE OF THE NORTH." IT IS IMPOSSIBLE TO KNOW WHAT THE BELGIAN SINGER AND SONGWRITER WAS REFERRING TO, BUT IT IS ONE OF THOSE THINGS THAT ARE IMPLICIT AND THAT ONE CAN SENSE. CERTAINLY, IT IS EASY TO PROVIDE AN ALMOST ANATOMICAL DESCRIPTION OF THE GEOGRAPHY OF MOROCCO: THE RIF MOUNTAINS ARE THE HEAD, THE ATLAS MOUNTAINS THE STOMACH, THE ATLANTIC AND MEDITERRANEAN ARE THE SIDES, AND THE DESERT PLAINS ARE THE LEGS AND FEET THAT EXTEND AS FAR AS ALGERIA, MAURITANIA, AND BLACK AFRICA. BUT LET'S BE SERIOUS—A COUNTRY IS NOT A POSTCARD. NOR IS IT A MERE COLLAGE OF PHYSICAL ZONES THAT ARE MORE OR LESS SPECTACULAR AND THAT VARY IN POPULATION. A COUNTRY IS A COMBINATION OF HISTORY,

20
The cold water of the Atlantic washes the splendid red
sand beaches, giving rise to intriguing formations.

Introduction

CULTURE, ADAPTATION, AND APPARENTLY INVISIBLE ELEMENTS. IT IS A MOOD, ONE COULD SAY. AND, INTERESTINGLY ENOUGH, IN MOROCCO ONE CAN PERCEIVE THIS EVEN WHEN FLYING AT AN ALTITUDE OF 3300 FT (C. 1000 M), SUSPENDED IN A POCKET OF HOT AIR THAT COMES FROM THE DESERT, OR JOLTED BY THE FURIOUS WINDS OF THE ATLANTIC COASTS.

THE LANDSCAPES CHANGE RAPIDLY AND ARE NEVER THE SAME. THE MOUNTAINS SWELL INTO TWO, THREE OR FOUR 'TAXIWAYS' OF RIDGES AND PLATEAUS, AND THE PLAINS EXTEND AS HUGE GREEN EXPANSES BEFORE GIVING WAY TO THE MONOTONE AND DISTURBING SAHARAN REGIONS. AND YET ONE FEELS THAT IT IS PRECISELY IN THIS SEEMING CONFUSION THAT THE MOROCCO OF GREAT CONTRASTS TAKES ON FORM: "A COLD COUNTRY," SOMEONE ONCE SAID, "WHERE THE SUN IS WARM," COMPRISING RICH AND POOR, MODERN AND ARCHAIC. HERE IT IS THE HOME OF THE SEMI-NOMADIC SHEPHERDS, AND FURTHER ON ARE THE BERBER FARMERS, DETERMINED TO MAKE THEIR FIELDS FERTILE AND NOT ALLOW THE SAND TO GAIN THE UPPER HAND. ONE SENSES THE SOCIAL CONFIGURATIONS THAT MUST REGULATE THE RELATIONSHIPS AMONG THOSE WHO GROW UP IN THE MIDST OF THE THOUSAND ALLEYS OF THE

Introduction

MEDINA IN FÈS OR TÉTOUAN; THE FATIGUE OF THOSE WHO RESIST THE TORRID HEAT AND DROUGHT IN SMALL AND LARGE OASES WHERE EVERYTHING IS PRECARIOUS, CHANGEABLE, AND TRANSITORY; AND THE SOCIAL AND CULTURAL PHENOMENA THAT ARE TRANSFORMING THE LARGE URBAN AREAS, THE INTERPRETERS OF A YOUNG MOROCCO THAT HAS GREAT RESPECT FOR THE PAST AND EXPECTATIONS FOR THE FUTURE, AS WELL AS A NATURAL PREDILECTION FOR THE HERE AND NOW. *CARPE DIEM!* LONG LIVE THE PRESENT.

THIS IS MORE THE METAPHYSICS OF SPACE THAN THE AESTHETICS OF GEOGRAPHY, BECAUSE MAGIC IS LIKE COOKING: IT IS A QUESTION OF PROPORTIONS. AND THERE IS MORE THAN ENOUGH IN THE LAND THAT THE ANCIENTS CALLED THE MAGHREB, THE WORLD OF THE SETTING SUN. A FASCINATING LAND THAT WAVERS BETWEEN THE WEIGHT OF TRADITION AND THE DESIRE FOR CHANGE. RECEPTIVE AND HOSPITABLE TO STRANGERS, YET RESERVED, JEALOUS OF ITS VALUES AND CLINGING TO CUSTOMS THAT HAVE PASSED THROUGH GENERATIONS APPARENTLY WITHOUT BEING CONTAMINATED. THANK GOODNESS! IT IS THE CONTRASTS THAT SHAPE OUR PERCEPTION OF THIS STRIP OF MEDITERRANEAN AND ATLANTIC AFRICA, WITH ITS TALL

Introduction

MOUNTAINS AND VAST DESERTS, ARID AND FERTILE, ARAB AND BERBER, AND NOT ON-LY DUE TO THE SYMBOLIC FRUSTRATION OF A LAND THAT SEEMS EAGER TO MERGE WITH EUROPE BUT CANNOT MANAGE TO BRIDGE THE NINE MILES, THE FIFTEEN KILO-METERS OF PHYSICAL AS WELL AS CULTURAL DISTANCE THAT SEPARATE IT FROM SPAIN AND GIBRALTAR. EVEN THE YOUNG KING MOHAMMED VI RECENTLY ADMITTED THIS: "FOR WESTERNERS MOROCCO IS THE ORIENT, AND FOR ORIENTALS IT IS THE WEST." THUS THERE IS STRIKING CONTRAST BETWEEN THE GLAMOUR OF CITIES SUCH AS MARRAKECH AND ESSAOUIRA, WHICH HAVE BECOME THE LATEST HAUNTS OF MIL-LIONAIRES FROM HALF THE WORLD, AND THE HARSH ESSENTIALITY OF A RURAL BERBER WORLD THAT HAS NOT YET TASTED THE ADVANTAGES OF AN ECONOMIC BOOM THAT SEEMS TO FAVOR THE ARABS WHO LIVE ALONG THE COAST.

IT DOESN'T MATTER THAT MUCH. THE STRONG CONTRASTS INDUCE A SLOW RHYTHM, DESPITE THE FACT THAT LOW-COST, LAST-MINUTE AND ALL-INCLUSIVE OF-FERS FROM TRAVEL AGENCIES SEEM TO STIMULATE FAST-PACED, SUPERFICIAL VACA-TIONS. BECAUSE THE TRUE JOURNEY DOES NOT CONSIST IN GOING TO NEW SET-TINGS AND LANDSCAPES, BUT IN OBSERVING IN A PARTICULAR FASHION. AND THIS IS

Introduction

ALMOST A CATEGORICAL IMPERATIVE IN MOROCCO, A COUNTRY EASY TO EXPLORE BUT ALWAYS A LAND OF ADVENTURE, BOTH PHYSICAL AND INTERIOR, WHICH DOES NOT FRIGHTEN OR DISTURB ONE BUT WHICH CAN BE LIKENED TO ANYTHING EXCEPT A TOUR-OPERATOR'S PROMOTIONAL BROCHURE. FLYING OVER ESSAOUIRA IS LIKE ACTIVATING A TIME MACHINE. THIS WAS THE AREA VISITED BY A LARGE NUMBER OF PERSONS OF THE SO-CALLED PEACE AND LOVE GENERATION THAT IN THE 1960S AND 1970S WENT WILD OVER PAUL BOWLES, CAT STEVENS, JIMMY HENDRIX AND BRIAN JONES AND THAT WENT TO MOROCCO CONVINCED THAT IT WAS THE LAST UTOPIA OR PARADISE. IN A FEW HOURS' TIME ONE FINDS ONESELF AMONG THE VALLEYS AND CANYONS OF OUARZAZATE, WHERE RIDLEY SCOTT, DAVID LEAN, MARTIN SCORSESE AND TONY SCOTT SHOT SOME OF THEIR MOST MEMORABLE FILMS, BRINGING WITH THEM SUCH FAMOUS STARS AS SEAN CONNERY, MICHAEL CAINE, GÉRARD DEPARDIEU, BRAD PITT, ROBERT REDFORD, AND MICHAEL DOUGLAS TO MOROCCO AND FILLING THE LANDSCAPE OF THE SOUTHERN REGION WITH PAPIER-MÂCHÉ BACKDROPS, AS IF EVERYTHING WERE A SCREENPLAY, THAT IS TO SAY, FICTION. WHICH IS NOT SO BAD, AFTER ALL, SINCE THE CINEMA FILLS LIFE WITH DREAMS.

Introduction

AND IN MOROCCO IT FILLED THE AREA WITH TENS OF THOUSANDS OF WALK-ONS, TURNING AN ARID PRE-SAHARAN REGION INTO A LUXURIANT 'HOLLYWOOD OF SAND.'

IN THE VILLAGES OF THE HIGH ATLAS MOUNTAINS ONE FINDS THAT THE JOY OF THE BERBERS IS EQUALED ONLY BY THEIR FRUGALITY. AT ZAGORA YOU COME UPON LITTLE ALADDINS WHO ARE ONLY TOO HAPPY TO EXPLAIN THAT TIMBUCTU LIES ALMOST A TWO-MINUTE WALK FROM THEIR GRANARY. AND AT JEMAA-EL-FNA YOU RISK A SEIZURE OF AGORAPHOBIA. THIS IS A THEATRICAL, 'FAR-OUT' LOCALITY THAT THE LAST STORYTELLERS AND SINGERS ARE TRYING TO SAVE FROM THE BANALIZATION OF MASS TOURISM AND COMMERCIAL AGGRESSIVENESS AND THAT UNESCO HAS PLACED ON ITS 'WORLD ORAL HERITAGE LIST,' USING IT AS A PRETEXT TO EXTEND OVER THE ENTIRE PLANET A NEW FORM OF INTERVENTION: THOUGHTS, TALES, MUSIC, CULTURE, IN SHORT, EVERYTHING THAT IS IMMATERIAL AND INVISIBLE, IS TO BE CONSIDERED A HERITAGE THAT MUST BE PROTECTED. BECAUSE, AS VICTOR HUGO SAID, WORDS ARE LIVING BEINGS. AND PERHAPS SO ARE THE MEMORIES OF THE MANY IMPORTANT PERSONS WHO LEFT THEIR HEART, AND SOMETIMES LOST THEIR HEAD, AT MARRAKECH: CHURCHILL AND MAURICE CHEVALIER, JOSEPHINE BAKER AND PIER PAOLO PASOLINI,

Introduction

JOE COCKER AND ZEFFIRELLI, JEAN-PAUL GAUTHIER AND MARLON BRANDO, CHARLIE CHAPLIN AND RITA HAYWORTH. WHICH IS BETTER, TO SAY THE LEAST, THAN DORIS DAY AND JAMES STEWART IN THE FILM *THE MAN WHO KNEW TOO MUCH*, A TALE ABOUT THE KIDNAPPING OF THEIR SON AMID SPIES, CORPSES AND INTRIGUES. NO NEED TO WORRY, THIS WAS ONLY ANOTHER INSTANCE OF FICTION AND FANTASY. ALFRED HITCHCOCK HAD TO LOOK FOR SNAKE CHARMERS AND FIND MERCHANTS WHO LOOKED SINISTER, SUCH AS THE SERVANT WHO IN THE FILM WHISPERS SOMETHING IN STEWART'S EAR. YEARS LATER, THE MORE OBSERVANT SPECTATORS RECOGNIZED THIS CHARACTER AT ONCE: HE HAD BECOME THE MAÎTRE OF THE MOST STYLISH RESTAURANT IN THE MYTHICAL MAMOUNIA HOTEL.

AMID CONTINUOUS BENDS, CURVES AND CHANGES, ONE MAY FIND ONESELF BEWILDERED, AT A TOTAL LOSS. BUT IN MOROCCO THERE IS NO DOUBT THAT A STRAIGHT LINE IS RARELY THE BEST WAY TO GET TO KNOW A COUNTRY. IT IS MUCH BETTER TO CONFRONT THE HIGH PASSES, GO THROUGH THE VALLEYS, LEAVE BEHIND A BEAUTIFUL IMPERIAL CITY WITH THE KNOWLEDGE THAT ELSEWHERE THERE ARE OTHERS THAT ARE NO LESS BEAUTIFUL. AND, IF POSSIBLE, READ THE EXTRAORDINARY TALES OF

FLYING HIGH MOROCCO

Low houses and narrow alleys characterize the towns
in the province of Marrakech.

MOROCCAN AUTHORS SUCH AS TAHAR BEN JELLOUN, MOHAMMED CHOUKRI AND AB-

DELKÉBIR KHATIBI, WHO HAVE ALREADY CAPTIVATED THOUSANDS OF EUROPEAN READ-

ERS WITH THEIR STORIES, WHICH ARE NOT TRUE BUT OFTEN QUITE PLAUSIBLE.

AND NOW, AFTER SO MANY COMMAS, WE COME TO THE FULL STOP. HAPPINESS IS

ARRIVING AT TANGIER, SIPPING A MINT TEA AND WATCHING THE SUN SET. BUT THIS IM-

PLIES TURNING YOUR BACK ON THE STRAIT OF GIBRALTAR, THAT IS TO SAY, EUROPE,

WITH ITS CERTAINTIES AND ITS OBSESSIONS. KEEP YOUR GAZE FIXED ON THE SOUTH,

ON AFRICA THAT BEGINS HERE AND ENDS HERE, WITHOUT EVEN HAVING TO DEAL WITH

THE BOTHERSOME EFFECTS OF JET LAG OR THE DISCOMFORT AND INCONVENIENCE

OF INTERMINABLE LONG-DISTANT FLIGHTS. BECAUSE, AS THE FRENCH SAY, MOROCCO

IS LA PORTE À COTÉ, NEXT DOOR.

30-31
The Middle Atlas is a patchwork of pastures and small plots of cultivated land.

32-33
Turquoise and ocher merge in the coastline west of Ceuta, where the Atlantic penetrates the Mediterranean.

34-35
The colors of the desert become spotted with white in the salt flats of the Laayoune area.

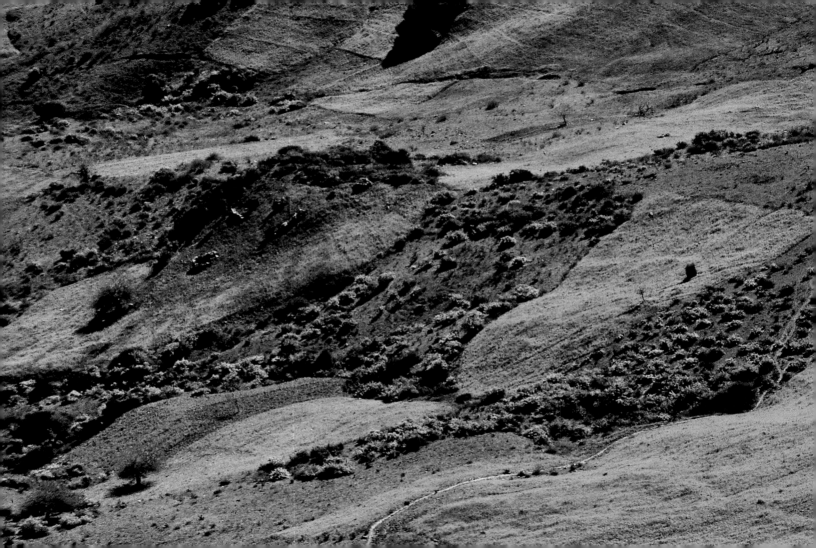

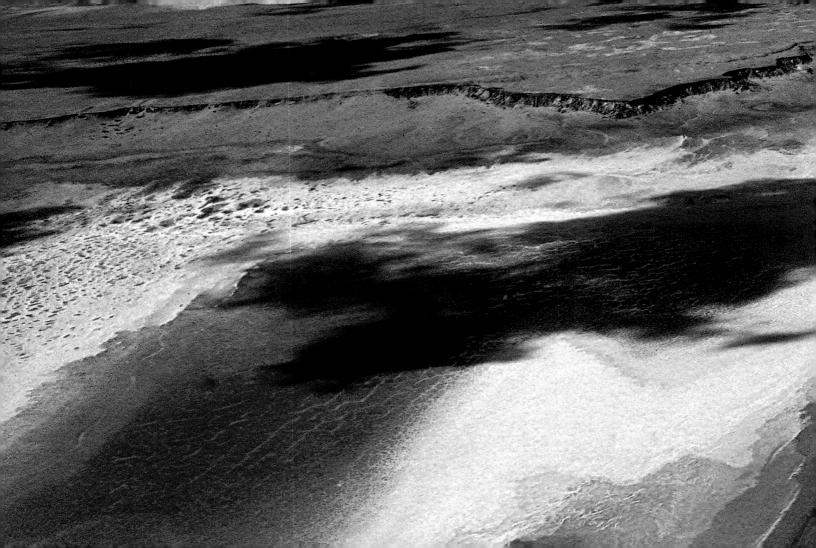

DUNES THAT SING, OASES THAT LIVE

Flying High

FLYING HIGH MOROCCO

37

At Laayoune, the ocean of dunes and its wide range of colors.

38

In southern Morocco the landscape is dominated by the warm colors of the Erg Lehoudi.

The inertia of the village. In Morocco one always heads south, to Ouarzazate, Tinerhir and Erfoud, because the Sahara stirs the imagination of travelers and evokes a certain idea of primordial humanity, of our lost infancy, of inviolate nature. This is an attraction that materializes by moving from one place to another, simulating brief forms of nomadic life. Because hiking in the sand is like walking in the snow: one leaves footprints. Except that here we have to reckon with the first sandstorm, which will arrive suddenly, hiding all traces of humankind and its mindless vanity.

The lines of the horizon vanish in the infinite, all perspective is distorted, and humans become heroic figures, miraculously capable of making the most arid land fertile. And in the meantime the Dades Valley continues onward, with villages that have the same color as the earth and cultivated fields that are divided into square farm areas in order to better exploit the available water. And dozens of kasbahs along the sides of the valley, fortified citadels that dot the land, crowned by towers and covered with terraced roofs, the austere appearance of which is relieved somewhat by the occasional decorative motif. An imperative is to stop along the Ziz River valley in order to observe and meet the inhabitants of the oases, who dedicate all their time to prolonging the fragile existence of the palm trees. Another must is to descend into the Tafilait zone, where wells line the streets, almost as if to protect them from erosion. Again, you will realize that the lake that appears a short distance from Merzouga is not a mirage, if only because you will see birds that make a stop there during their long migrations.

Stones, nothing but stones. One could say this is desert land, and basically this is true. The rivers are bone dry for the most part, their beds mere fossils of torrents that manage to be so in more than name only during the tumultuous but occasional rainstorms. And the ocean of sand is finally nearby, although it is not boundless like the Ténéré desert in Niger or the Tanezrouft in Algeria. In any case, the Erg Chebbi desert is a foretaste, a sampling, a synthesis. And magic is an automatic occurrence here, where the dunes are shaped like long, curved croissants that lie perpendicular to the dominating wind.

Dunes that Sing, Oases that Live

It is impressive and at the same time reassuring, accessible, almost domesticated. And it does not matter much if it seems to be besieged by the four-by-fours that start off from the Dar Kaoua oasis and then head for the village of Khemliya, on the south side of the Erg: they stop a short distance away to avoid being sanded, and this in itself is a good thing.

And if the supreme luxury were precisely this empty space? A tent and a camp are worth as much as all the five-star hotels in the entire universe. And what does it matter if your thin mattress is not too comfortable and that it is hard to tell the difference between the dunes that the wind has compacted and hardened and those that are less exposed, in which one inevitably sinks? The desert is an exercise in slowness and perseverance. What is essential are the vault of the sky, the absolute, the immensity, the Milky Way and the stars that seem to shine so much more brightly. In the daytime one has to find out whether the sand really sings, as the great travelers claim. It depends on the sun and wind. In certain conditions the dunes emit a sound that can be heard for miles and miles and that reminds one of the sirens' song. Whether

this is suggestion or something else, who knows? Further on, a short distance from Taouz, are the borders that mark the beginning of Algerian territory, amid large boulders that are black because of the torrid climate and colored dunes in the Hassi Ouzina and Tafraoute area, so rich in 'desert roses,' the crystalline lamelliform rocks sold by the locals who for the same price offer improbable but entertaining explanations of their origin. But once here you find there are very few traces of the mythical desert city of Sijilmassa, which in the 7th century was considered a sort of metropolis, an obligatory stopping place for the trans-Sahara caravans that once transported gold, ivory and slaves. Then there is the Draa River valley further west, which brings with it the water and greenery from the spurs of the Atlas Mountains, a veritable highway of water and oxygen that slackened the thirst of caravaners for centuries and now satiates the fantasy of photographers and travelers, who are seduced by a river that appears and then disappears in the beds of impressive canyons among the Siroua and Saghro hills, finally coming to an end among the dunes that mark the Algerian border. But before fading away, this waterway

Dunes that Sing, Oases that Live

feeds fertile oases and gardens in areas that are crossroads of various peoples–Arabs and Berbers, people with European features and descendants of the black slaves who once arrived here from distant Timbuktu after fifty or more days' travel on dromedaries, as is recorded in a naif graffito situated at a junction of Zagora, the only road leading to the spurs of the Anti-Atlas and further south, up to the arid stretches of the Western Sahara, among Guelmin, Laayoune, Smara and Dakhla. A life experience and lesson. One becomes aware of everyday things thanks to a sort of sensorial metamorphosis. Or perhaps it is only because the space is different, the light is something else again, time is lengthened. One has the feeling of being stripped bare, of having got rid of all superfluous weight, of thoughts becoming lightened. And one discovers that the desert in Morocco is inhabited – by populations that have adapted to the environment in order to survive, by simply amazing fauna and flora, by unbelievable creatures, by the historic memory carved in thousands of rock paintings. We return to the asphalt road, which at this stage is like traveling on a freeway. Here again are the dunes of the great South that move, or better run, where they shouldn't. The power lines become like Ariadne's thread at Knossos, in a landscape in which perspective seems to have been abolished. And there are barriers of palm trees replanted in order to check the desertification: they offer the locals what they need to survive: wood to warm themselves in the winter or to make roofs for their homes, dates to be eaten or exported, and even the base used to distill its lymph and produce alcohol. Local philosophy: tomorrow will be better than today. And this must be true, since the new economy is developing side by side with the arrival of vacationers and globetrotters. When things go wrong there is always a zaouia, a sanctuary, where one can receive the protection of a local saint or solicit aid from some confraternity in the Tamegroute area, the last real urban settlement in the Saharan province, with a library founded in the 17th century by an erudite traveler, Muhammad Ben Nacer, that is crammed with manuscripts on astrology, Koranic law, literature and philosophy that the dry climate has preserved in remarkable fashion. A metaphorical site in the south of Morocco: those who travel in the desert seek the void; those who live in it seek to fill it.

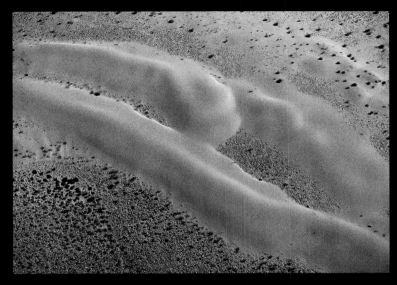

42 and 43
Very few people, an expanse of sand on a sea of stone, and very little vegetation: the Jebel Ougnat personifies Morocco, with its feet in the desert.

44-45
Like nearby Mt Saghro, the Jebel Ougnat is the domain of the semi-nomadic Ait Atta: in the hot season they leave this area and head for the plateaus of the High Atlas, and then descend again in winter.

46-47
South of Guelmin is the es-Smara zone, the desert area that Morocco claimed as its own in the 1975 'Green March.'

48

Es-Smara, in the middle of one of the most remote regions in Morocco, is visited by thousands of Saharans every year for the festivities celebrating the end of Ramadan.

49

The same colors, similar villages, the same contrast between the ocher of the desert and the green hues of the small oases: the Jebel Ougnat almost touches the road that goes from Tinerhir to Erfoud and the Merzouga dunes.

50
For centuries the Aouinet-Torkoz oasis was used by caravans that traveled from the Sahara to the Atlantic coast.

51
The village of Aouinet-Torkoz lies at the foot of the Jebel Ouarkziz.

FLYING HIGH MOROCCO

53
Very few wells, the occasional village, tracks constantly buried under the sand: Aoui-net-Torkoz is emblematic of the Lower Draa River valley.

54
Small settlements in the village of Aouinet-Torkoz, at the southern end of Morocco.

55
The desert surrounding Aouinet-Torkoz is one of the last corners of Morocco where one can periodically spot gazelles, hyenas and felines.

56

The region south of Laayoune that extends toward Dakhla was accurately and poetically described by the French author Saint-Exupéry: "A blond expanse where the wind has manifested its power."

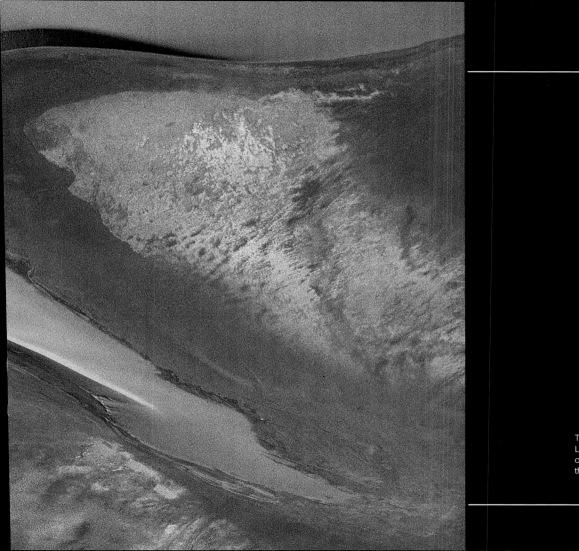

58-59
The sandy desert lies around Laayoune: the 'Tekna' nomads occasionally visited the region that extends as far as Guelmin.

FLYING HIGH MOROCCO

61
The interior of former Spanish Sahara is virtually without urban areas, but because of its phosphate deposits Laayoune is a strategic region for Morocco.

62
Laayoune developed in the vicinity of the mouth of the Seguia el-Hamra, the mythical river that has inspired many Moroccan and foreign writers.

64
Human presence is decreasing more and more, as many no-mads have abandoned the most remote regions and have gone to live in town, at Laayoune.

65
The desert landscape accompa-nies travelers along the road that runs from Laayoune to Dakhla, toward Black Africa.

FLYING HIGH MOROCCO

67
Swirls of dunes 'decorate' the hard and monotonous layer of the *hammada*, the rocky desert of the Sahara that extends as far as Laayoune.

68

The Laayoune region is the western side of the Morocco desert that to the East extends as far as the Tafilalt oasis.

69

Two small settlements near Laayoune that look like two presidios in an abandoned desert area where waiting in expectation can become disquieting.

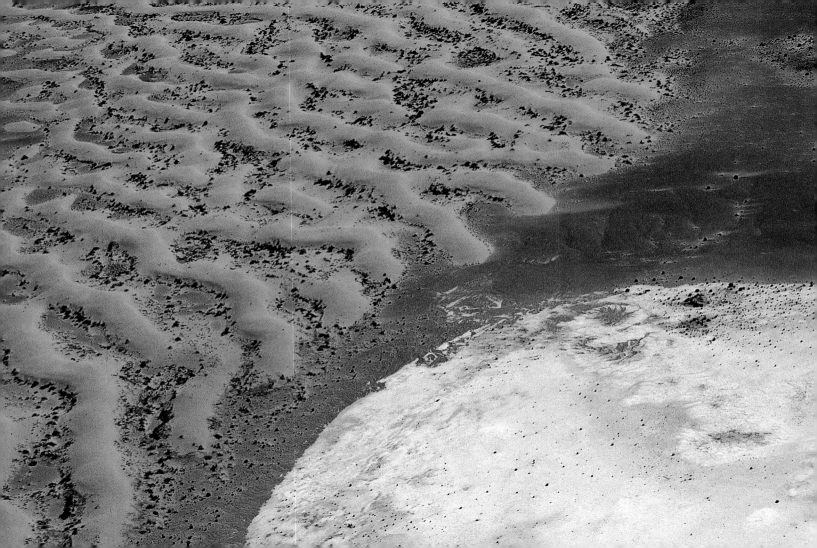

70
Extensive desert areas crown the Ziz River valley.

71
The desert region that begins at Tinerhir runs to the dunes of Merzouga, in the middle of the Sahara region.

FLYING HIGH MOROCCO

73
The stretch of the Western Sahara between the Atlantic coast and Taouz attracts a great number of lovers of fossils and meteorites.

74

The abandonment of the most remote areas of the southern desert surrounding Laayoune has contributed to the disintegration of many nomadic communities.

75

Many oases in the Moroccan Sahara around Laayoune are disappearing because of the inadequate management of the water resources.

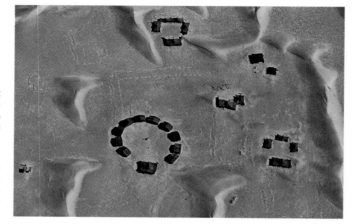

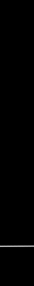

76-77
The void, or the Sahara around Laayoune. This is one of the least densely populated regions in Morocco, but is also the one in which the government is investing most.

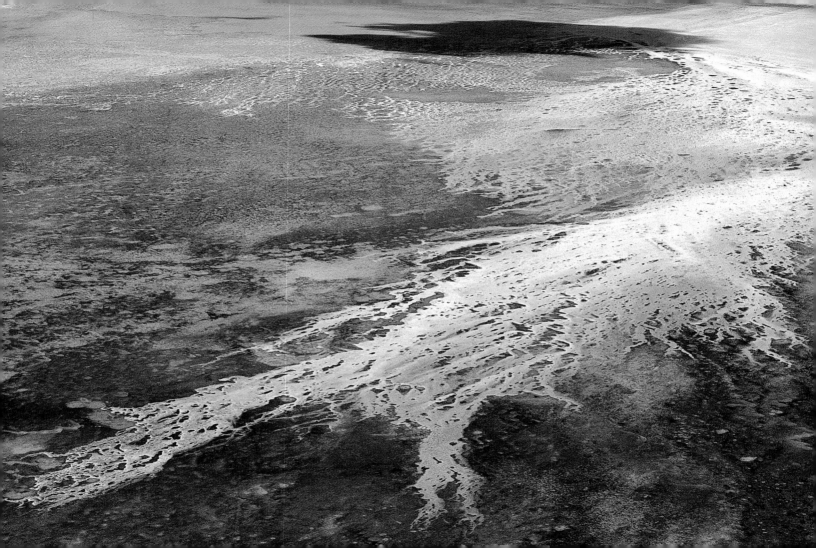

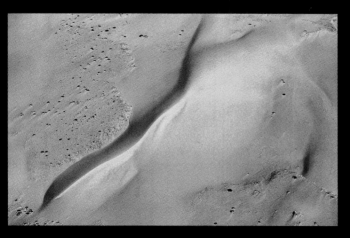

78
Lack of water is a major problem for desert dwellers between Laayoune and Es-Smara. The rare water sources one comes upon are in stark contrast to the saline expanse.

79
There is no longer any trace of the caravan routes that once passed near Laayoune and linked Black Africa with the Atlantic ports.

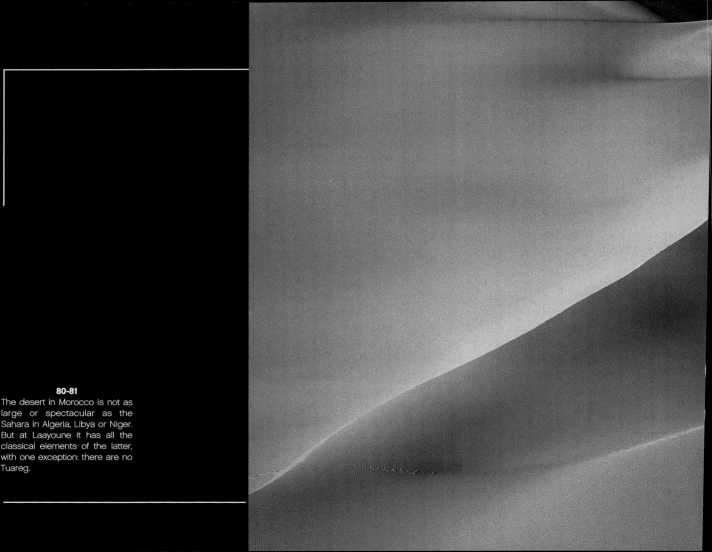

80-81
The desert in Morocco is not as large or spectacular as the Sahara in Algeria, Libya or Niger. But at Laayoune it has all the classical elements of the latter, with one exception: there are no Tuareg.

BETWEEN THE PILLARS OF HERCULES AND THE UNDERTOW OF TWO SEAS

FLYING HIGH

FLYING HIGH MOROCCO

83
A short distance from Melilla, many Moroccans have created small summer residential areas.

84
The Plage Blanche or white beach is a seemingly endless stretch of fine sand.

Never trust your first impression, not even when it concerns a cliché. Because the liquid element is to be found everywhere in a country that despite this likes to present itself as a land of solid things: snow-capped mountains, desert plateaus, mysterious medinas, fertile oases. There is water everywhere. An endless strip of coastline, almost 2236 miles (3600 km) long, starting off from here at the long beach at Saïdia, a town with a few bathing establishments more or less a stone's throw from the Algerian border. Here there is no such thing as anxiety, hustle or bustle. Silence is still a characteristic element on the Moroccan coastline facing the Mediterranean that extends as far as the charming and phlegmatic village of Al Hoceima and even beyond it, along the Côte des Rhomaras, amid small Portuguese forts, small coves and the Rif Mountains that descend precipitously to the sea, creating a long series of capes and peninsulas that the small and rather dilapidated National Road No. 6 barely manages to connect to one another.

An obstacle course, so to speak. But basically this is the feature of this northern area that is somewhat mar-

ginal and ignored to a certain degree, where the language of Cervantes is understood better than that of Molière, olive trees are more common than date palms, and the houses, plastered with turquoise and lapis lazuli hues, remind one of Granada, Seville and Andalusia in general. At the Grottoes of Hercules, 2.5 miles (4 km) south of Cape Spartel and about 10 miles (16 km) from mythical Tangier, legend has it that the Greek hero rested here before his titanic encounter with Antaeus, the son of Poseidon. He slashed the earth, thus separating Europe and Africa at the point now known as the Strait of Gibraltar, and on each of the two opposite shores he erected a pillar to mark the end of the known and possible world. Viewed from on high, the strait truly seems to be a margin between two pages. And behind it is the most approachable Mediterranean and also the warmest part of this sea, with an average temperature of 25°C and a high level of salinity. Opposite, toward Asilah and Larache, the Atlantic is more insipid and disturbed by upwelling, the phenomenon that causes the cold water from the depths to rise when the winds and the

Between the Pillars of Hercules and the Undertow of Two Seas

Earth's rotation pushes warmer water on the surface toward the open. Proceeding further, we are suddenly confronted with the ocean, which is harsh, at times inhospitable, despite the fact that this coastline, where the largest cities are located, is endless. One understands this from the long waves, the boundless beaches, the colder, darker hues of the water; the Marja Zerga bird preserve, 17,300 acres (7000 hectares) at the mouth of the Drader River, the home of storks, flamingos, and curlews; and the secret charm of Oualida, a bathing establishment between Casablanca and Essaouira, with dunes and fine sand beaches and a low tide that periodically reveals islets covered with greenery where cows can graze for a few hours before the high tide covers them all up once again.

Even further on, under Essaouira, Tafadna beach is framed by an arid region that is not good farmland; but the Berbers of Sous gather the strange fruit of the argan tree to extract oil that is used to make an ointment with medicinal and antioxidant properties and also as an ingredient in their local cuisine because of its vague pra-

line scent. In any case, this is better than at Tamri, where the dunes are shaped by the devastating erosive actions of the waves and the ocean periodically unleashes its rage and breaks the silence with the gloomy sound of its undertow. New investments are due to arrive in this area, which will not be the same in the near future. But if the desert beaches are a privilege, then this one is still a paradise, as surfing buffs seem to confirm. They wait for the tallest wave, ready to ride its crest before it crashes on to the shore, and take advantage of the direction of the trade winds that blow so hard here from March to September because of the thermal combination of the cold air of the ocean and the warm air from the interior. They perform yet another pirouette, hoping to end up among the legends of this sport immortalized in the surfing slicks. Speaking of legends, at Sidi R'bat the surfers literally crash onto the shore, exactly like the waves. Some people have said this was the setting for the story of Jonah and the whale, as well as of the Arab general Obqa Ben Nafi, who in AD 682 arrived on his horse and galloped toward the ocean,

Between the Pillars of Hercules and the Undertow of Two Seas

screaming that he would take Islam to every corner of the world. The fishermen, however, are satisfied with reality. They wait for spring to make up for the lean winter, a rough season for those who have to take to the open sea to find what they cannot find on the land. These are the whims of this grey sea lacking in tropical hues, colored only by the pinkish reflections of the flamingos that flock to the lagoons of the Massa and Sous rivers, vying for the available space with the cormorants, avocets, cranes, grey herons, and the extremely rare *Geronticus eremita* ibis with a bald head, dark feathers and rather ugly appearance that ornithologists avidly search for at the break of dawn and try to immortalize as if it were the only purpose in their life. We descend once again, as if drawn by the magnetic power of the most secluded and remote regions of this country, forgetting how long it takes to get past Mt Tiznit by car, and head to Goulimine and Tan-Tan, along a road that every so often seems to lose its bearings in stretches of desert, while other times it becomes a corniche or coastal road that skirts interminable white and ocher beaches. Like the ones that lead to the gigantic natural bridges made of red rock hewn by the water and wind at Legzira, a short distance from Sidi Ifni. Or those that run around the lagoon of Khnifis in the Tarfaya area, formerly a way station for the Aéropostale or air mail planes, where the French author and traveler Antoine de Saint-Exupéry used his pilot's license to become an adventurer of the skies along the first transcontinental airplane routes. This was the starting point, in November 1975, of the so-called green march promoted by King Hassan II to regain the 'Sahara provinces' and impose sovereignty on what the Spanish once called the Rio de Oro. The fact that this is a separate world is borne out by the shepherds' camps, the towns surrounded by walls to protect them from sandstorms, the frequent checks made by the nomad police, the old garrisons of the Foreign Legion converted into settlements for thousands of Saharawi nomads who have become sedentary, more or less integrated, and more or less happy, through the influence of time and life. Because in the desert one learns to adapt: sometimes out of opportunism, almost always out of necessity.

88-89
The coastline of eastern Morocco, overlooking the Mediterranean, the last part of which ends at the Algerian border.

90-91
Lovely sand dunes facing the sea with its beautiful colors: this is the typical scenery of the coastal Rif area, in the vicinity of the mouth of the Moulouya River.

FLYING HIGH MOROCCO

93
Many lakes are artificial, created to support agricultural development in the area where the Moulouya River flows into the sea.

94
A long succession of capes and promontories lines the Rif coast, in the vicinity of Melilla, the largest Spanish enclave in Africa.

95
The asphalt road connecting Nador and Melilla cuts through a frontier that has often been the cause of tension between Morocco and Spain.

FLYING HIGH MOROCCO

97
A spectacular beach near Nador, a locality where tourism is still scarcely developed.

98

Negotiable roads that run through the Rif area and head toward the Mediterranean coast are rare indeed.

99

Along the most remote stretch of the Rif coastline are the beautiful beaches of Ariet Arekmane and Cap des Trois Forches.

100-101
The impressive stretch of road
that goes to Cabo Negro, also
known as Ras Tarf, near Tétouan.

102
The so-called Fishermen's Cape is like a large hump. For a few *dirhams* one can go on an organized boat tour around this cape.

103
Turquoise water and long beaches lie at the end of the Rif valleys that descend to the sea.

104
Along the so-called Côte des Rhomaras the Rif Mountains plunge into the sea, making one long for the endless sandy beaches of Al Hoceima and Saïdia.

105
To the west of El-Jebha is the craggy Côte des Rhomaras, the land of famous Berber leaders. One of them, Abdel-krim el-Khattabi, headed the war the Rif region waged against the Spanish and French troops in the 1920s.

106-107
An impressive cliff at Fishermen's
Cape, a sort of Cape Horn facing
the Mediterranean.

108-109
Fishermen's Cape is a rugged, barren crag whitened by the sun; seems to thrust itself into the sea. It owes its name to the nearby small fishermen's villages that still live off the rich waters of this part of Morocco.

110 and 111
The barren scenery that runs from the interior toward the coast is typical of the area facing Spain.

112
In the 1980s and 1990s the beaches south of Tétouan were very popular with tourists. Now tourism seems to prefer the localities to the East, at Saïdia.

113
Impressive lush vegetation lends its rich green hues to the coast connecting Cap Malabata and Ceuta.

114

A long strip of asphalt skirts the Mediterranean coast toward Tangier. According to legend, the island of Calypso, the nymph in Homer's Odyssey, was located in this region.

115 left

Many towns dot the Moroccan coast facing the Strait of Gibraltar.

115 right

Fishing is the main activity of the people who live in the coastal region east of Cap Malabata, facing the Strait of Gibraltar.

116 left
New towns in the province of Tangier. The mythical city of northern Morocco is passing through an active phase of revival after years of neglect and decline.

116 right
The final stretch of the road that comes from Ceuta and Tétouan: this is the largest gateway to the city of Tangier.

117
The last fine sand beaches on the Mediterranean: Tangier is a stone's throw away, as is the Atlantic.

118-119
As one heads toward Asilah, the Atlantic coast appears to be less rugged and barren than the one in the Rif region.

120

The Asilah zone is traversed by torrents and rivers that originate in the western section of the Rif range.

121

Irrigated fields and arboriculture: agriculture is one of the mainstays of the economy of the region facing the Atlantic.

122-123
Toward Larache the monotony of the long strip of sand along the Atlantic coast is broken up by promontories and rock formations.

124
The area along the Atlantic coast a few miles from Larache is a favorite haunt of ornithologists and bird-watchers because of the Moulay Bousselham and Merja Zerga lagoons.

126-127

At low tide the lagoon that flanks Oualidia reveals its treasures: tongues of white sand that paint the turquoise sea, and interesting flotsam scattered along the watermark.

128
The economy in the Oualidia area is based on intermittent income from agriculture and oyster farming.

129
To the south of El-Jadida the sandy coast sets off plots of land used for market gardening.

130
The rivers and torrents that flow into the sea form evocative round lagoons whose color ranges from navy blue to turquoise-green.

131
The beaches around Oualidia are very crowded in summer, when the number of residents passes from 10,000 to 30,000. In low season the coast becomes 'wild' once again.

132
The thick network of cultivated fields is the backdrop to the southern
coast of Oualidia.

133
The mysterious lagoon of Oualidia is not the Camargue region in
southern France, but it is closely resembles it.

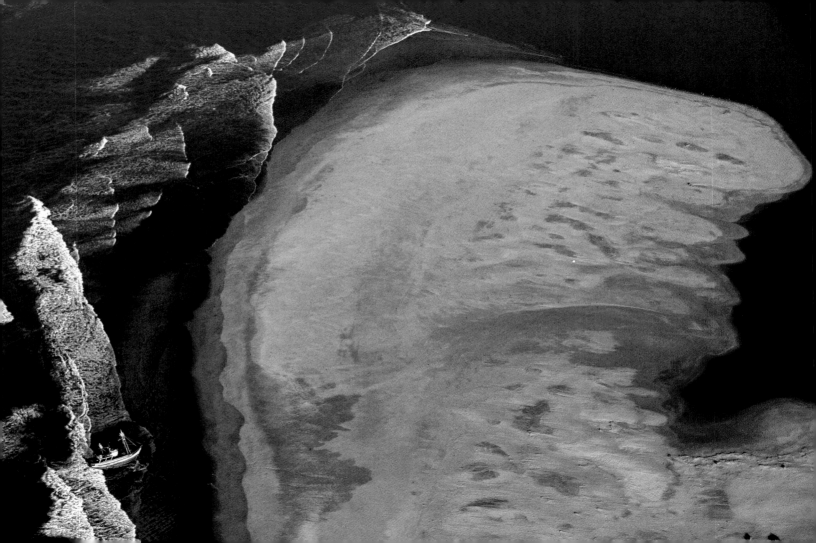

134
The dreams of development in tourism between Essaouira and Agadir have not been realized; for the most part the coast is still virgin and the beaches seem deserted.

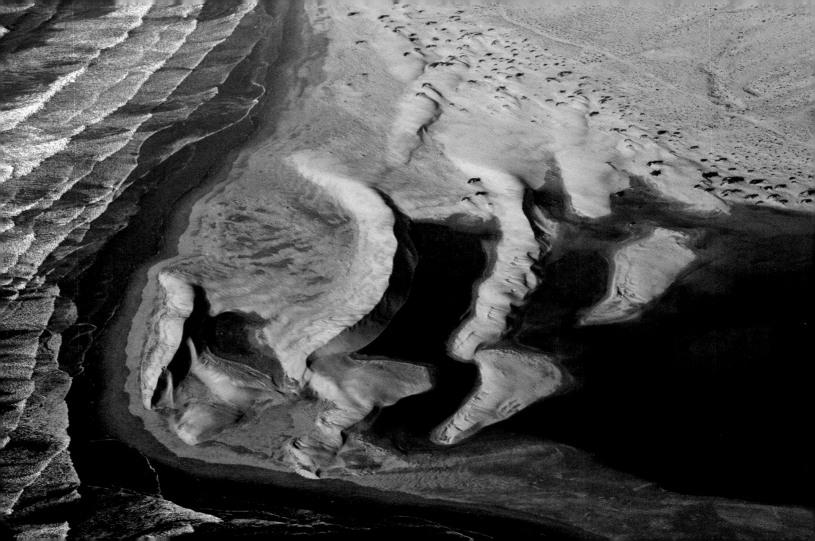

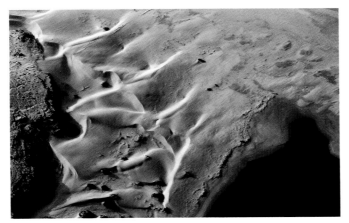

136
The central coast of Morocco, especially the area south of Essaouira, is a favorite with surfers.

137
The wind and tides have shaped the landscape of the inner coast of Agadir.

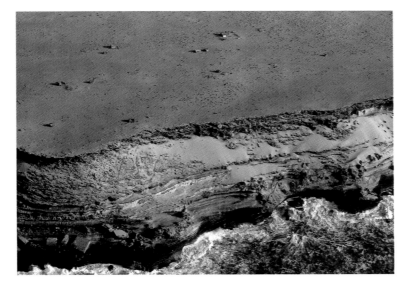

138
The beaches along the Atlantic around Agadir are impressive but have the drawback of a strong undertow.

139
The large dunes in the Agadir area are subject to the erosive action of the Atlantic.

140-141
South of Essaouira the Atlantic
coast is a continuous alternation
of limestone cliffs and sand.

142
The coastline north of Agadir is studded with rocky promontories
around Les Roches du Diable (The Devil's Rocks).

143
Small communities dot the coast. The Agadir region heralds the great
arid South.

144
The *taros*, the violent winds that blow from the end of March to early September around Essaouira and Cap Sim, are a deterrent to the development of large towns.

145
Thousands of migratory birds nest in the cavities of the cliffs among the beaches of Tafadna and in the ornithological preserve of Imzi.

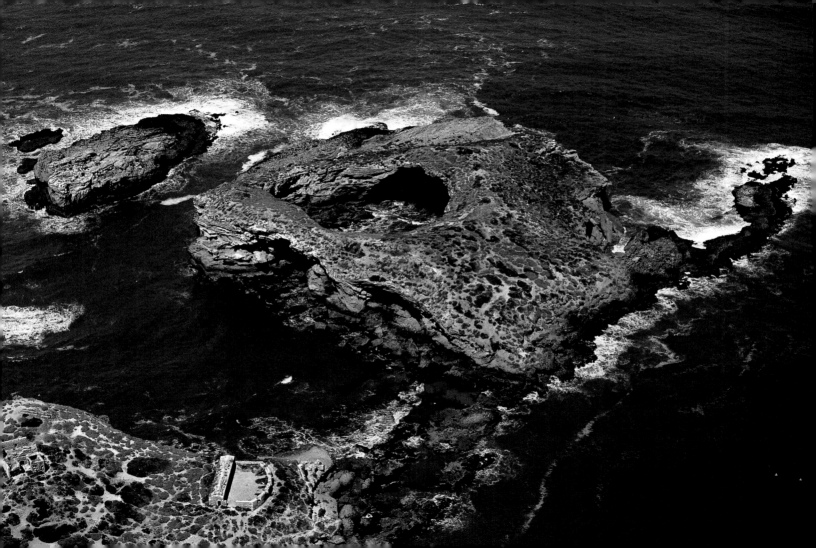

146
Residential complexes and vacation homes have favored the development of seaside tourism at Agadir.

147
One of the splendid coves that dot the coastal region of Sous.

148
The northern coast of Agadir has tiny coves with small fishermen's villages.

149
The Atlantic coast of Morocco around Agadir often has natural scenery with large cliffs plunging headlong into the rough sea that remind one of similar landscapes in Northern Europe.

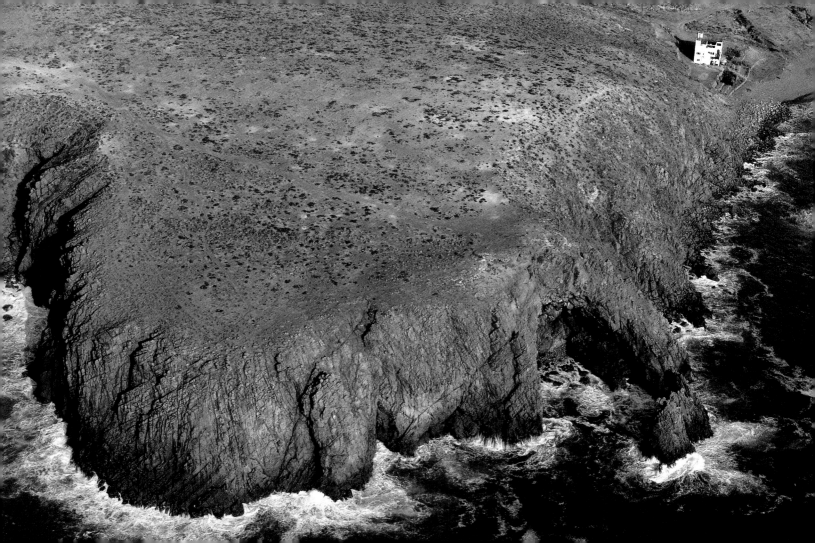

150
The Atlantic coast in southern Morocco is always pounded by violent waves.

151 left
The abandonment of the rural areas has also struck some zones near Agadir.

151 right
The National Road links the southernmost part of Morocco and the large coastal cities in the North.

152
The bright colors so typical of the pre-desert region of Sidi Ifni are a great attraction for travelers.

153
Old French redoubts in ruins and abandoned villages dot the coast between Tiznit and Sidi Ifni.

154-155
Vast beaches around Sidi Ifni –
another paradise for surfing
buffs.

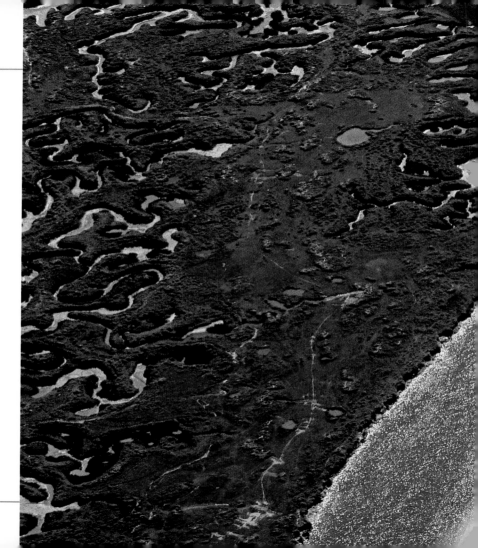

156-157
In the past the Draa River marked the exact border between the French and Spanish protectorates.

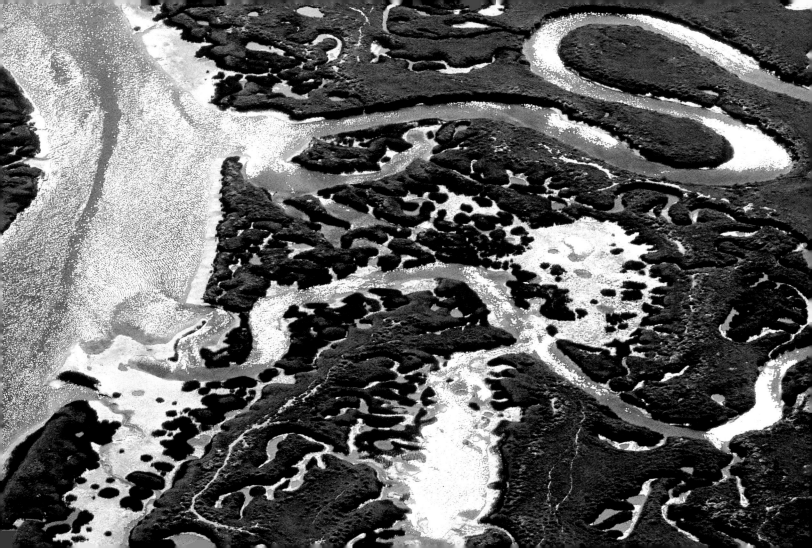

FLYING HIGH MOROCCO

159
The Plage Blanche extends for about 37 miles (60 km) along the coast north of Tar-faya. This is an uninterrupted sandy belt with unique natural features, on which only one hotel and a few fishermen's huts reveal the discreet presence of humankind.

160
The desert and mineral landscape is the backdrop to the interminable Plage Blanche.

161
Mythical Cap Draa was named after the long river that originates in the High Atlas, even though most of its water is swallowed up by the desert before arriving at the sea.

FLYING HIGH MOROCCO

163
The seemingly endless National Road that runs from the North to Laayoune before the last stretch, which leads to Mauritania.

THE CITIES OF KINGS AND STORYTELLERS

FLYING HIGH

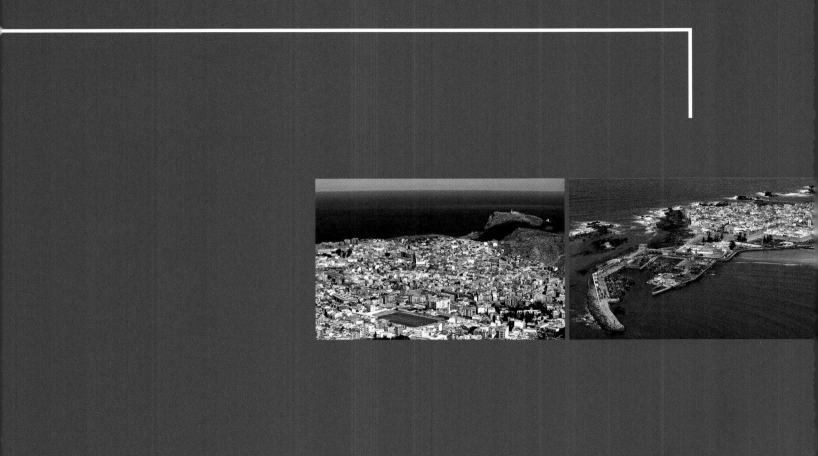

FLYING HIGH MOROCCO

165
Al Hoceima (left) and Essaouria (right) have an important historic and artistic heritage.

166
The old city of Asilah evokes the splendor of the ancient Carthaginian port.

167

Pretexts and priorities. There is always time to organize an excursion to the Atlas Mountainss. or camping in the Sahara Desert. In order to understand Morocco it's better to be in a crowded place, like the cities. They are books to be leafed through, read, and interpreted: the squares are pages, the alleyways are block letters, the houses are words.

For example, there is Fès, with its narrow streets one can hardly pass through, souks moth-eaten like rugs that someone must mend sooner or later, buildings in good condition and others that are in a bad state, waiting for funds that the World Bank and UNESCO have allotted so that they do not disintegrate.

The ideal thing would be to visit the fountains dressed in polychrome tiles; take lodgings in a foundouk or old caravanserai that with time has been converted into a small hotel; and, from the top of a minaret, admire the panoramic view of this wonder of town planning that the Marinid sultans achieved when they made it their capital, filling it with royal palaces and religious and Islamic law schools, gardens and fountains, almost as if they wanted to recreate the Andalusia that was so dear to them. In the end, you are quite happy to enter one side of the medina and end up on the other side, in order to grasp the sense of a city that rigorously respects the political and economic hierarchies and understand something more about the architecture, which is pervaded with the symbolic relationship bet ween the square and circle, the columns and vaults, the earth and sky.

Time flies. There is Tétouan to the north with a medina that is a labyrinth of winding alleys with a Mediterranean atmosphere. There is Meknès, which Ishmail, second sultan of the Alawite dynasty, transformed into the heart of the Moroccan kingdom, in other words, an imperial city, to the detriment of its direct rivals, Marrakech and Fès. And there is also Rabat, the present-day, modest capital of the new kingdom that a grandiose new town plan hopes to transform into a small, dynamic metropolis but that continues to hark back to the operetta-like aspect of the old town, a fortified citadel that was once the republic of corsairs more interested in organizing raids than cultivating good taste and wisdom.

Essaouira faces the same ocean from inside its massive ramparts, like a Saint-Malo transplanted in Africa, battered by the strong, constant wind that brings good thoughts and sweeps away the bad ones. Every summer the town comes alive with a Woodstock of hybrid sounds invented by the 'Gnawa' masters, and ancient Mogador becomes a Puerto Escondido for thousands of Westerners with emotional crises and in need of clear, fresh air.

Perhaps the oxygen is necessary in order to deal with tentacular Casablanca, the driving force and showcase of Morocco, the city of surreal town-planning experiments, with Neo-Moorish buildings side by side with Art Déco architecture, nondescript working-class quarters, elegant villas in the upper-class district of Anfa and modern towers like those of the Twin Center designed by the Catalan architect Ricardo

Bofill. One promenades along the seafront lined with fashionable cafés, small restaurants with a Latin atmosphere, and the gigantic Hassan II Mosque, built on a strip of land reclaimed from the sea. This is the largest mosque in the world after the one in Mecca, with a 690-ft (210-m) minaret that emits a laser beam that can be seen 18 miles (30 km away, for the glory of Allah and those who constructed it. Somewhat like what happens in white Tangier, perched on the crest of Africa, its feet in the Mediterranean and Atlantic, in that hybrid and tormented 'transit station' that the ancients considered the end of the world and that modern dreamers think is a magical place of inspiration and perdition: afflicted by troubles but now full of promise as well. Tangier will shine as much and even more than before, justifying the gigantic investments that have been made to turn it into the largest and most international port in Morocco. We must the update the guidebooks: the ugly duckling is becoming a swan.

The epilogue is at Marrakech, and it is even better

The Cities of Kings
and Storytellers

than the prologue. Because it is here that the human comedy is on stage every day, in the large open space of the medina that the conteurs, the last of the bards, are trying to save from the banalizing effects of movie houses. The oblique light of sunset kindles the Jemaa-el-Fna esplanade, a place with vague borders that seems to be chaotic and anarchic but is really regulated by rules, taboos and customs. It is a vast crossroads that has no profile even though we think we see it, a transit area where speeches are made and listened to, where the singular becomes plural, and where the hours are linked to a precise function: mornings are for traversing, afternoons for strolling. Two or three hours are enough to change the colors, the scenario, the plot and even the mental attitude here. At night one is less watchful and excesses are forgiven. You linger in front of some elderly persons who do a takeoff on life and human shortcomings in an imperial city that is a conglomeration of wealth and misery, fatigue and luxury, houses in which promiscuity is a condemnation and magnificent riad or palaces with Arab-Andalusan decoration inhabited by VIPs and new tenants, foreigners who can afford to buy everything and have few rivals in this enterprise.

An endless sequence of images: the circle of storytellers, the *halqa*, a small yet grand geometric composition that may refer to the cycle of the Sufi or the whirl of those mystical dancers, the dervishes. Then there are the 'in' spots, the exclusive meeting places of bohemians, 'neo-hedonists,' vacationers, slaves to fads; the walls of the houses covered with *tadlakt*, whitewash smoothed and colored with beige and vegetable dyes that make the walls look as smooth as shiny as marble; and the markets where the locals can see what the superficial travelers are unable to note because they are distracted by all the tourist souvenir junk on display.

A parody of life and human shortcomings. Absurd and chaotic, natural and real. Marrakech becomes the epitome and metaphor of the Moroccan cities, which seem like circles of Dante's *Inferno* but are pleasant, human, biodegradable.

Saïdia

170-171
Situated along the Algerian border, Saïdia overlooks the Mediterranean near the mouth of the Moulouya River, the last stretch of which consists of lagoons and marshes.

172

A major town in the north of Morocco, Nador has many examples of Andalusian and Neo-Moorish culture. Many streets and squares have
plaques and signs in both Arabic and Spanish.

173

Nador has a gridiron layout and is heavily industrialized. Its fortune is
linked with that of nearby Melilla, one of the last Spanish enclaves in
Africa.

Nador

175
The name Al Hoceima supposedly derives from the Arabic 'Al Khozama,' or 'lavender,'
a tribute to this city, which in fact becomes bluish-purple at sunset.

Al Hoceima

176
The suq still has some scars left by the earthquake that struck the Rif region in February 2004, but it is nonetheless the most exotic and popular spot in Al Hoceima.

177
Al Hoceima boasts two beautiful beaches with golden sand and an endless series of coves that are often deserted even in high season, a situation that will not last for very long.

FLYING HIGH MAROCCO

178
Compact and homogeneous, Al Hoceima is perched on a horseshoe-shaped cliff overlooking the Quemado beach.

Tangier

180-181

A crossroad between Africa and Europe and between the Mediterranean and Atlantic, Tangier boasts all the fascination of intriguing, mysterious, romantic and depraved cities. For many years it was the hub of displaced persons, spies and adventurers.

182-183

Tangier, the most European of Morocco's cities, is also the most cosmopolitan and unconventional. In the 1950s the American author William Burroughs, along with other exponents of the Beat Generation, described the restless and anxious spirit of this city.

184

The fascinating bay of Tangier has seduced painters, composers and other creative persons. Henri Matisse – who upon his arrival there exclaimed: "Paradise exists!" – depicted it in one of his most famous watercolors.

185 left

Detached from the country's economic life for years, Tangier is now the hub of gigantic investments. In a few years the grand Tangier-Med project will be finished, creating one of the largest international ports in the Mediterranean.

185 right

Modern buildings and hotels overlook the beach on the bay. For the moment somewhat neglected and underdeveloped, this promenade may soon become the showcase of Tangier.

186 and 187

Asilah recently revived its former splendor and its *medina* is among the best kept and preserved in all Morocco.

188-189

Fishing and pleasure boating: Asilah is attempting to improve its economy by developing its seaside resources as well.

Asilah

190
The series of towers and bastions built by the Portuguese military architect Botacca in the 1500s surrounds the *medina* of Asilah.

191
Squares that remind one of arenas, white houses with blue or green shutters, wrought-iron balconies: there is an air of nostalgia in the streets and squares of Asilah, as the architecture bears evident traces of Portuguese and Andalusian influences.

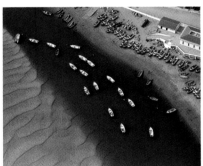

192

Refreshed by the ocean spray, Moulay Bousselham comes alive only in the hot summer, when it becomes its real self, so to speak: a small provincial city with its feet in the Meja Zerga lagoon and in the Atlantic.

193 left

The lagoon is a great resource for the local economy. Daily life at Moulay Bousselham is marked by the rhythm of the boats going to and fro between the gloomy waters of the ocean and the inner beaches of the bay.

193 right

Every July thousands of worshippers throng the mosque and tomb of Moulay Bousselham, the local saint who died in the 10th century.

Moulay Bousselham

194
The Bou Regreg River in the middle and on either bank two cities that have always been light years apart as far as character is concerned: Rabat, the vain and pampered capital of Morocco, and industrious, working-class and handicrafts-oriented Salé.

Rabat

196 and 197
The large open space separating the Hassan Tower, the Mohammed
V Mausoleum and the mosque opens onto a inner courtyard framed
by arches. This is the most monumental part of Rabat.

FLYING HIGH MAROCCO

198
From the top of its 12th-century mud walls, Rabat keeps watch over the mouth of the Bou Regreg River, the base of the pirates who terrorized the Mediterranean coast until the early 19th century.

Casablanca

200

With a population of almost three million, Casablanca is the largest city in Morocco, the country's only true metropolis.

201

The immense Hassan II Mosque – which can accommodate more than 20,000 worshippers – and its 689-ft (210-m) minaret dominate the oceanfront of Casablanca.

202
The commercial wealth of Casablanca has always revolved around its
port, one of the most modern and active in Africa.

203
The Hassan II Mosque was constructed in the 1990s to celebrate the
former king of Morocco. It is the second largest mosque in the world,
only the one in Islamabad is bigger.

205
Rare ancient Roman ruins contrast strikingly with the modern aspect of Morocco's economic capital. Casablanca cannot match the rich historic and artistic heritage of Morocco's other cities: it is a modern metropolis in which districts inspired by Western architecture alternate with nondescript outskirts with dilapidated buildings.

206 and 207
Tourism and seaside residences flourish around Casablanca: small villas overlook the ocean, while a short distance away beaches with golden sand are thronged nine months a year.

FLYING HIGH MOROCCO

209
The paving outside the Hassan II Mosque is made up of different types of fine marble laid out in the geometric patterns typical of Islamic art. Over 60,000 persons can congregate in this square, and the interior can house 20,000 during the liturgy. This mosque was finished in 1993.

210

Enclosed within massive bastions, El Jadida "the Portuguese," as it is called, is one of the most photogenic cities along the Atlantic coast.

211

Once known by the Portuguese name Mazagan, El Jadida was rebuilt and modernized in the first half of the 19th century. It is on the UNESCO World Heritage list.

El Jadida

Safi

212 left
Located at the end of a superb coastal road, Safi has a large port used for the fishing industry and the export of phosphates.

212 right
Crescent beaches herald the charm of Oualidia, a town that is a favorite with the Moroccan middle class.

213
The 'sea castle' of Safi, a small fortress overlooking the ocean, opens out to the north through an old entrance surmounted by Portuguese emblems, since in the 16th century the edifice was the governor's residence.

FLYING HIGH MOROCCO

215

Founded by the Carthaginians, Essaouira boasts ancient commercial traditions that made it a major port of call on the route to the Gulf of Guinea. The 'golden age' of Essaouira was in the 19th century, when merchandise brought via the caravan routes was loaded onto the ships. An offshoot of Casablanca, Essaouira is now a picturesque marina and fishing port.

Essaouira

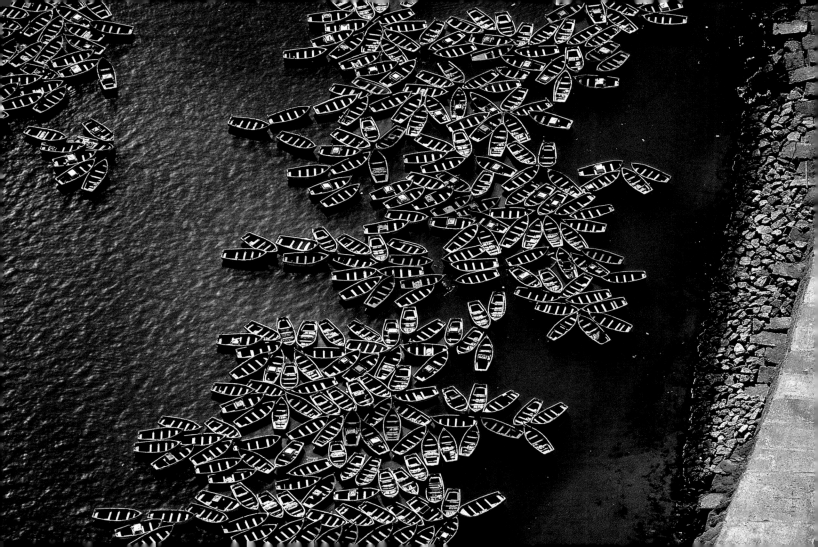

216 and 217

In the early 1970s, thousands of hippies thought they had found the setting for their utopia in front of the fishermen's harbor of Essaouira.

219

Present-day Agadir has been developed in the last forty years to replace the old town, which was founded by the Portuguese in the 16th century and destroyed in 1960 by two tremendous earthquakes. Among the attractions are the active fishing harbor and the extensive beaches with fine sand.

Agadir

220
The principal economic center in the Sahara provinces, Laayoune is a city that is rapidly expanding, partly due to the large areas in the vicinity where phosphates are extracted.

221
One of the large squares around which extends Laayoune's commercial zone; straight streets and houses that are generally low and often have domed roofs.

FLYING HIGH MAROCCO

222
Laayoune grew up on the mouth of the Seguia el Hamra River and is a point of interchange with the Saharawi nomads who live in the region.

Oujda

224 left
A huge city-market, Oujda is a very lively commercial town that handles products from Rif, the Middle Atlas and the desert region of Figuig.

224 right
Large spaces and squares: the new quarters of Oujda have grown so much that they now infringe upon the *medina*, both in terms of space and importance.

225
Oujda is the capital of the northeastern regions of Morocco and one of the obligatory stops along the road and railroad that connect Casablanca and Algier.

226

A transit point of major roads and railway lines connecting Fès with Oujda, Taourirt has become the refuge of many immigrants from the nearby rural regions.

227

Taourirt, in Morocco's eastern region, is one of the largest and most important cities along the so-called Taza Corridor, which links Morocco and Algeria.

Taourirt

228
At the crossroad between northern and central Morocco, Ouezzane is
surrounded by hills that extend into the mountainous zone of Jebala.

229
The natural gateway to eastern Morocco, Taza was a major military
stronghold during the rule of the Almohad dynasty.

Ouezzane and Taza

FLYING HIGH MOROCCO

231
A cultural and gastronomic capital, Fès is the oldest of the four imperial cities and is the third most important city in Morocco. Here we see the old town, rich in historic buildings, markets and mosques, which make it one of the most fascinating places in the entire Islamic world.

Fès

232 and 233
The enigmatic and mysterious *medina* is a labyrinth of alleys, narrow streets and courtyards. According to legend, the ancient capital of the Marinid dynasty kings stood on the exact perpendicular of Paradise.

234-235
Fès is made up of three distinct sections: Fès el Bali is the *medina*, Fès el Jedid is the imperial city, and further south is the new town, which was built during the protectorate period.

236-237
The area around the bastions of Fès is dotted with cemeteries, many of the tombs of which date to the Marinid dynasty.

238
The mausoleum of Moulay Idriss, the founder of the first Moroccan state and the country's most venerated saint, dates back to the 18th century and is always filled with worshippers. However, entrance is forbidden for non-Muslims.

239
A university city, one of the holy cities of Islam, and formerly the capital of the Moroccan sultanate, Fès gradually lost its important role. During the period of the French Protectorate, new, Western-type quarters were built there.

240

During the reign of Moulay Ismail, in the period bridging the 17th and 18th centuries, Meknès enjoyed its golden age, becoming the capital of the kingdom. This was the period of the construction of the loveliest quarters and the walls of the present-day city, which now has a population of over 500,000.

Meknès

M'rirt

242
M'rirt is a large town about thirty kilometers from the city of Khenifra.

243
M'rirt is situated over 3280 ft (1000 m) above sea level on a broad plateau in the Middle Atlas. It owes part of its development to the mineral deposits in the Jebel Aouam area.

Khenifra

244-245
Khenifra, on the road that links Fès and Marrakech, is part and parcel of Moroccan history, as it was one of the cities that most fiercely resisted French dominion.

246

The site of battles (in 1907 the Moroccan rebels fought the French troops here), Tamelelt is a lovely town at the edge of the desert, with an Arab atmosphere, narrow streets, and low houses with terraced roofs and courtyards shaded by the many typical Muslim gardens.

Tamelelt

248
Marrakech is a large city with Islamic traditions. It has many minarets that rise up over the roofs, the most famous of which is the one on the Kutubiya mosque (12th century).

249
Now a metropolis with almost one million inhabitants and an international airport, Marrakech is considered the gateway to the Moroccan Sahara.

Marrakech

250
The Menara Gardens are one of the symbols of Marrakech. The pavilions and extensive olive orchards make up an area of greenery with warm hues in this city near the desert.

251
At the edge of its large residential district, Marrakech offers enchanting views, including the Agdal and Menara gardens, large and peaceful areas ideal for picnics, the large lakes and the cool shaded zones.

252

Djemaa el-Fna (above) is the square around which the old town de-
velops and is usually considered the hub of Marrakech.

253

The ancient capital of Marrakech was 'discovered' by Europeans who
were attracted by its fascination and lively inhabitants, but the city has
preserved its Arab character, which can be noted in the suqs and upper and lower *medinas*.

FLYING HIGH MOROCCO

255
The second largest city in Morocco, Marrakech is not only a fascinating center of Arab culture. Over the years it has acquired – at least in the most recent districts – a modern look that is also European to some degree, as can be seen in the large avenues.

256 and 257

Tinerhir is a bright pink-ocher city dominated by the ruins of an old fortress and closed off to the north by the Todra gorges.

258-259

Built around a rocky spur that towers over a large palm tree grove, Tinerhir marks the boundary between the valley of the casbahs and the desert region of Tafilalt.

FLYING HIGH MOROCCO

261
Along the so-called Valley of Marvels is the village of Ait Benhaddou, an important stop along the ancient caravan route that started at Marrakech and penetrated the desert. The fortified town, used as a setting for some famous films (from *Lawrence of Arabia* to *Alexander*), it is now almost completely abandoned and has been placed on the UNESCO World Heritage list.

Ait Benhaddou

262
Some 124 miles (200 Km) south of Marrakech, Ouarzazate is the true gateway to the great South, at the intersection of the High Atlas and the desert regions.

263
The central section of Ouarzazate is dominated by the Taourirt casbah, formerly the summer residence of the pashas of Marrakech and the heart of a Berber village before the construction of the new town.

Ouarzazate

264
Only an hour's trip from Agadir by car, Taroudant is a lovely town at the
foot of the High Atlas; it is completely surrounded by high walls.

265
Taroudant is considered half a city and half an oasis because of the famous orange and pomegranate gardens inside splendid Arab courtyards.

Taroudant

266 and 267

Situated in the Draa River valley, Zagora is the last, authentic city before the expanse of dunes, the terminal of an asphalt road that about 18.5 miles (30 Km) farther on gives way to difficult tracks.

Zagora

IN PRAISE OF VARIETY AND DISORDER

FLYING HIGH

FLYING HIGH MOROCCO

269

All the colors of the rainbow can be seen by traveling from the province of Marrakech (left) to Ouarzazate (right).

270

The Oued el Makhazine Dam provides a large supply of water and energy to north Morocco.

"God created countries with a great deal of water so that people could live in them, and deserts so they could recognize their souls." A wise saying, like all Berber proverbs. It is by no means easy to regard a country like Morocco solely as a physical entity, a merely geographic space where people can theoretically be ignored. But while this may be a somewhat ill-considered and audacious abstraction, it is nonetheless excusable in this part of Africa that is not immense but where nothing is uniform and everything exists side by side with its opposite: aridity and fertility, oases and desert, plains and mountains, dry torrents and those that periodically swell like rivers in Amazonia and rush down toward their natural destination–the sea, the ocean.

This is a world that must be seen and admired. Better yet, since we can now count on good cameras and aerial photographs, we can section the landscapes, recompose them, as it were, thanks to the magic of overflight. In this way the whole becomes the sum of its details and there is nothing better in this country, which has the rare gift of synthesis: an endless maritime façade, four different massifs, fertile plains, valleys that may look like stigmata, holes in Swiss cheese, or small Edens, and a desert that every so often is nothing but deep sand but that also takes on the form of impressive canyons, extremely barren plateaus, stretches of meteorite-like land that remind one more of lunar landscapes than the more classic ones of Saharan dunes.

A eulogy of variety and disorder. Here there is a physical and environmental chaos that is in contrast with the monotony and uniformity typical of other pre-desert regions in North Africa, and that makes Morocco one of the Mediterranean countries richest in biodiversity. With scenery that is so unpredictable

In Praise of Variety
and Disorder

that one's imagination tends to soar, and people actually give names of living creatures to the stones, peaks and valleys. Rocks that look like huge reptiles, summits that remind one of amphibians, cliffs similar to a dromedary's hump or head. And then parables are used to explain the geography and place names of the land. This is all quite normal: in Morocco they say that people can speak to each other from one mountain to another but that it then takes a half-day's walk for them to meet and finally shake hands.

Here one often ends up going uphill; more than a choice, it is an automatism. Because at high altitudes there is less oxygen but it is of higher quality, the air is tonic, the light is not ruined by humans and pollution. Herodotus wrote about this as long ago as the 5th century BC when he discussed the ends of the known world at that time and mentioned mountains so high that the peaks were invisible. This was

the Atlas group, and it was precisely Morocco that extends between the Mediterranean and the Atlantic Ocean in an interminable succession and superposition of landscapes. There is the Rif range to the north, a complex and barren series of mountains blanketed with cedar and oak, between the Strait of Gibraltar and the Algerian border. And there is the Middle Atlas, a system of chains and plateaus that divides the country into a western meseta and another one to the east, a plateau dotted with conical rises and hills that look like overturned teacups, an area periodically frequented by semi-nomadic shepherds because of the rather thick vegetation.

The High Atlas is not far away – mighty and massive, an ecological niche that has the most important and interesting Berber communities in the world and offers a foretaste of the Anti-Atlas and the Eldorado of tourists, hikers and mountaineers who for the moment are still discreet, reserved and respectful.

In Praise of Variety and Disorder

It is only right, after all, to have the highest regard for these splendid areas. And also to discover that this austere mineral world that descends toward the desert is also inhabited: by populations that have adapted to the environment in order to survive, by astounding fauna and flora, strange small animals, by a historic memory that materializes in the numerous caves covered with rock carvings, and by the stubby clay constructions that from time to time appear from nowhere like sentries, defensive fortresses against presumed enemies or crossroads for spices and the exotic.

An educational and enlightening trip, up to the great southern region that looks like a "world at the end of the world" with its North African features, the same extreme elements as in the Patagonian pampas: boundless space, human presence that thins out, the wind that sweeps everything away and at the same time leaves sand and dust in its wake. So

be it. Facing the Atlantic, Laayoune, a city far from everything but at the same time a paradigm of the new Morocco, is going through an economic boom. This small capital of a region rich in phosphate is the last stop for those who venture along the coastline that 310 miles (500 km) further on arrives at Mauritania, as if heralding Black Africa and the tracks that promise to reach mythical Dakar.

It is a well-known fact that at the end of a long journey there is a reward. And the Dakhla region rewards visitors with the last surprise, somewhat like a prize won for curiosity, tenacity, and stamina: a fauna preserve and an unpolluted coast that is the home of the last important colony of monk seals on Earth. The geographic and ethical moral of this story is that in the land where people have often waged wars and engaged in conflict in order to impose their sovereignty, nature fights one of its most determined and tormented battles.

274
The hilly Ouezzane region is a transition zone between the more barren Pays Jebala and the plain that extends as far as the ocean.

275
Small and isolated settlements dot a profoundly rural landscape; the Ouezzane zone has environments that are also typical of the mountainous Rif region.

276
The upper north of the Middle Atlas is characterized by the geological rift known as the Taza Corridor.

277
In the vicinity of Taza, the scenery has typical Mediterranean vegetation, with cedar and oak trees. In the Tazzeka National Park one finds almond and cherry trees.

278
The scarcity of water causes the few rivers in the Middle Atlas and Rif regions to dry up, only to swell up and flood during disastrous rainstorms.

279
Along the road that runs from Taza to Oujda the scenery becomes barren, taking on the characteristic appearance of the eastern regions of Morocco.

280
The land around the Oued el Makhazine Dam is marly, consisting of a mixture of limestone and clay, and often covered with wild vegetation.

281
The Oued el Makhazine Dam lies in the middle of the Larache region in northwest Morocco, which is traversed by numerous torrents that descend from the Pays Jebala.

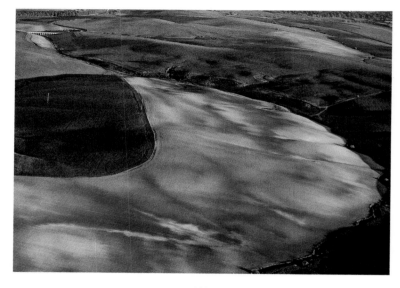

282
The rivers originating in the Middle Atlas have forged ravines and bends in the region around Fès.

283
The Fès countryside extends for miles over a rolling terrain marked by alternating cultivated fields and stretches of wild vegetation.

284
Geometrically arranged rows of trees bound the cultivated land in the
Fès region.

285
The fields around Fès boast some of the most beautiful citrus tree
plantations in Morocco; they are a complement to the traditional crops,
in particular cereal plants.

286
Farmland in geometric patterns: in the large Sebou River basin near Fès, agriculture is the mainstay of the local economy.

288
The massive dimensions of the Idriss I reservoir serve as a divide between the road that heads eastward and the one that runs to the Rif
region, that is, to the north.

289
The Oued el Makhazine dam prevents flooding of the plain that extends from the city of Ksar el Kebir to the Atlantic coast.

FLYING HIGH MOROCCO

291
Wedged among the Middle Atlas Mountains, the Idriss I reservoir has a dam dozens
of feet high.

292
The Idriss I 'barrage' has a capacity of 1,182,000 cubic meters of water and is located in a region considered the richest in this resource in Morocco.

293
The inhabitants of small villages live off the olive trees and kitchen gardens irrigated with the reserve of water provided by the dam.

294
A torrent in the Middle Atlas winds its way through the barren landscape of the Fès area.

296-297
The crests of the hills are covered with lovely greenery only a few dozen miles from Fès.

298-299
Volubilis, 18.6 miles (30 Km) north of Meknès, is the most important archaeological site in Morocco. UNESCO placed it on its World Heritage list.

300 left
In the second century AD Volubilis had a population of 20,000 and prospered thanks to olive oil, corn and animal husbandry. The ancient Romans constructed baths, triumphal arches and elegant buildings there.

300 right
The Triumphal Arch made of marble is the most impressive monument in Volubilis. It is the gateway to the main city street, the Decumanus Maximus.

301
The so-called Basilica, which once housed the courthouse and the trade market, is flanked by the Forum, the large central square of Volubilis.

FLYING HIGH MOROCCO

303
Some farming communities in the Ifrane and Azrou area extend in the shape of a swollen circle that is divided into sections so that the farmers and their fields can be connected.

304
A long embankment cuts through the hinterland of Casablanca.

305
The Middle Atlas offers many combinations of woods and farmland. For example, the main cedar forests are located in the Ifrane–Azrou–Khenifra triangle; farther west, these areas, in which olives and cereals are cultivated, are divided into plots.

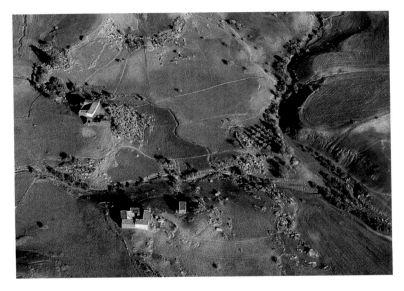

306
A dry river leaves marks that look like gashes in this lunar landscape
a few miles from the metropolis of Casablanca.

307
In recent years, the rural zone of Khenifra was the object of many projects offering credit to support agricultural and handicrafts activities. Despite this, the tiny villages in this region are gradually being abandoned.

308-309
Two-thirds of the population in the Chaouia Ouardigha region live in rural areas. But, as this photograph shows, more than half the territory uncultivated.

FLYING HIGH MOROCCO

311

In 1578 the surroundings of Ksar el Kebir, in the province of Boulemane, were the theater of the famous Battle of the Three Kings, which paved the way for Spanish dominion of Morocco and Portugal. In gorges such as this one, the Oued el Makhazen, 40,000 soldiers, the king of Portugal, the former king, and the sultan of Morocco all lost their lives.

312-313
The El Errabia River descends from northern slopes of the Middle Atlas and washes the plateaus between Khenifra and Beni Mellal before flowing into the Atlantic south of Casablanca.

314 and 315

The presence of the El Errabia River does not necessarily mean that the plains south of Khenifra are fertile. Winding its way for 372 miles (600 km), this is the second longest river in Morocco and has a discharge of 4230 cu. ft (117 cu. m per second). In order to reduce its water flow, no fewer than eight barrages were needed; these have allowed the locals to irrigate the plains of Tadla and Abda-Doukkala.

316
The slopes of the Middle Atlas create the corrugated terrain of Beni Mellal, in the heart of Morocco.

317
The spurs of the Middle Atlas frame the plain around Beni Mellal, the 'orange capital.'

318-319 and 320-321
Although the terrain is quite barrens at the foot of the Atlas Mts., many forestation and horticulture projects are underway in the vicinity of Beni Mellal.

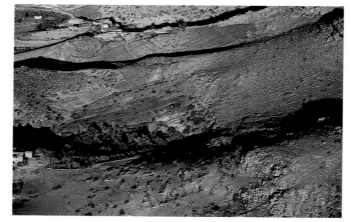

322
Lying in the middle of fertile land, the small villages make it possible
to optimize the natural resources and favor exchanges in the agricultural region of Beni Mellal.

323
The fertile plain south of Beni Mellal, along the road to Marrakech.

324

The Beni Mellal region is attempting to persuade the younger generation to remain by offering young people work and salaries that compete with those in the large industrial areas of Casablanca.

326 and 327
On the road to Safi, a stone's throw from the sea, small grassy plots of land are used as pasture for sheep and goats. The calcareous land is also used to cultivate a type of onion that, because of the chemical composition of the soil and the vicinity of salt water, has a particular, highly appreciated flavor. This area has a very small population.

328-329
The Bin El Ouidane 'barrage' is over fifty years old and is fundamental for the arboriculture and the cultivation of the fertile land between Beni Mellal and Tadla.

330
The villages south of Marrakech were the first to adopt measures to prepare for the first, and rather timid, forms of tourism.

331
The sandstorms that arrive from the Sahara Desert often strike the hilly regions and the plain that lead to Marrakech.

332-333
Marrakech is framed by many small oases that are like gateways to valleys of the High Atlas and Anti-Atlas.

334
For centuries the Berber populations have plowed the land that extends toward the Anti–Atlas.

335
The use of clayey material for building houses creates a strong effect of camouflage, and the villages blend in with the landscape.

336-337
The boundary area between the plain of Marrakech and the western slopes of the High Atlas is a true greenhouse of wild herbs and medicinal plants.

338
The mud dwellings in the El Mansur Eddahbi area remind one, on a smaller scale, of the so-called *ksar*, the fortified villages in the neighboring regions, the Draa River valley and the Dades River valley.

339
Because of its fertile soil the Marrakech region is one of the most densely populated in Morocco.

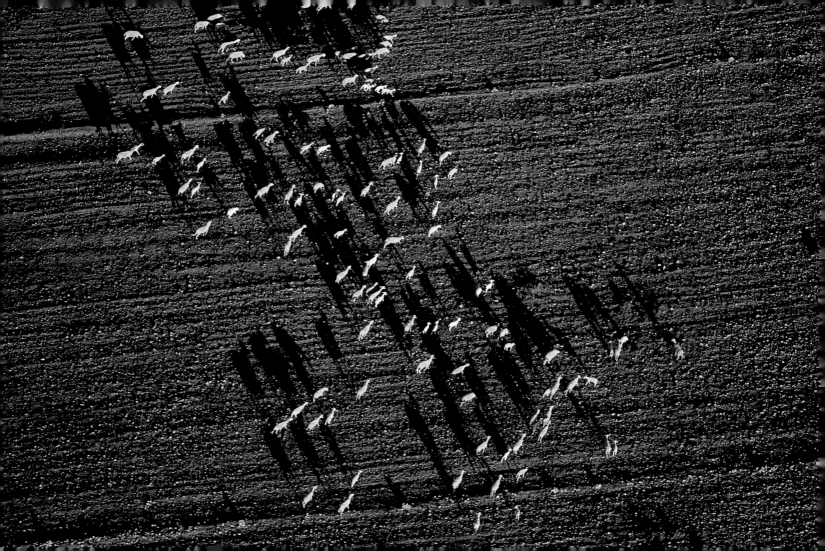

FLYING HIGH MOROCCO

340
Animal husbandry complements agriculture in the more isolated areas around Marrakech.

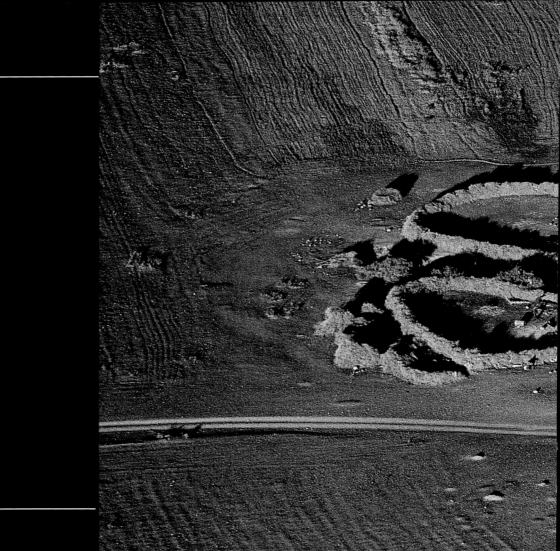

342-343
The small rural communities in the zones south of Marrakech must often face the serious problem of drought.

FLYING HIGH MOROCCO

345
Seasonal rains in the High Atlas area overlooking the plain of Ouarzazate favors the growth of small woods and limited urbanization.

346-347
Spectacular canyons are a backdrop for the El Mansour Eddahbi
reservoir, a small part of which is
seen at left.

348
The El Mansour Eddahbi Dam channels almost 785 million cu. yards (600 milllion cu. m) of water of the Oued Draa River into a reservoir and makes it possible to irrigate almost 24,700 acres (10,000 hectares) of land.

349 left
The south shore of the artificial lake near Ouarzazate is the least densely populated one.

349 right
The El Mansour Eddahbi Dam bounds the landscape between Ouarzazate and the Skoura oasis, with the High Atlas as a backdrop.

THE MOROCCO OF STRONG CONTRASTS AND BERBER LEGENDS

Flying High

FLYING HIGH MOROCCO

351

The Dades Valley (right) runs between the High Atlas and the black volcanic peaks of Mt Saghro (left).

352

The High Atlas is the highest mountain range in Morocco, culminating in Mt Toubkal (13,664 ft/4165 m).

The words are strokes of a pencil on maps and the language is a compass: great and small alchemies of the uplands. In the land of the setting sun the mountains may be craggy, hostile, and rugged, but they are inhabited all the same. And the populations that live in them speak languages – Riffian, Tamazight and Tachelit – that curiously enough reproduce en bloc the complex mountainous configuration of the land.

The mountains are omnipresent. The folded, aligned and slightly oblique chains are separated by somewhat undulating regions known as meseta. These mountains are both physical barriers and the very bonding agent, so to speak, of Morocco. They divide the country diagonally, and also divide two oceans, one consisting of waves and water and the other made up of sand dunes – in other words, the Atlantic and the Sahara Desert. But they also constitute the physical and metaphysical land of the Berbers, with their dialects, their community feasts that celebrate the cycle of the seasons and harvests, and their taboos, both major and minor, which serve to strengthen and bind the social fabric and defend the population from unwelcome external intrusion.

This is a closed and touchy world, especially on the Rif massifs, whose centuries-old history has been marked by wars and where the cultivation of cannabis has often been the solution to sluggish and meager economic development, a curious reputation for this part of Africa between Bab Taza and Ketama whose landscape would almost appear to be Swiss because of its fir and pine forests, its groups of Alpine chalets, and the 'ridge road' that runs down toward Fès and the Middle Atlas Mts. like an asphalt belt, a transition zone between the Mediterranean regions and the great South.

Another world. The presence of the Barbary ape, a sort of North African macaco, lends an air of exoticism to this land that is covered with grasslands and

The Morocco of Strong Contrasts and Berber Legends

woods but is also porous, unable to retain rainwater and thus not a very suitable place to live in. So be it. There is Ifrane, which claims to be a winter sports resort, and the wild region of Foum Kheneg dotted with volcanic cones; there are the cedar forest that surrounds the Zad hill and the source of the Oum Er Rbia, the longest river in Morocco, which drains and absorbs all the water in the region, swelling until it reaches the open sea near el-Jadida.

Boundaries. Such as the Tizi Tichka Tizi-n-Test passes, which provide access to the Upper Atlas, the spectacular ridge of Morocco that is 500 miles (800 km) long and boasts a dozen massifs rising over 13,000 ft (4000 m) above sea level and about 40 peaks more than 9800 ft (3000 m) high that alternate with plateaus, irrigated terraces and deep valleys carved by the 'fossil' rivers that with rainfall may become impetuous waterways and then, because of the climate, remain dry for months on end.

You must keep your eyes wide open here in order to note the details among the alleyways of the mud-colored citadels that blend with the land. Because the bijoux, tattoos and costumes tell us everything about the men and women who wear them–their tribal origin, social status, and very destiny. And because the henné plant is much more than pulp that improves one's looks and slows down the marks of passing time: for the Berbers it also has the power to heal, purify, and protect one against bad luck. Imagination and optical effects are also part and parcel of the area around Ait el-Arbi, some 12 miles (20 km) north of Boumalne, in the deep Dades Valley, where the mountains have been sculpted by erosion, creating coiled rocks that everyone calls 'monkey fingers.' Or in the southernmost spurs, where the snow on the peaks of the High Atlas Mountains looks like a meringue crust and serves as a backdrop to the desert scenery, offering images that are unbelievable and usually contradictory as well.

The Morocco of Strong Contrasts and Berber Legends

The law of probability. The roads are often nothing more or less than backbreaking tracks that are virtually impracticable without an off-road vehicle because of the capricious high-altitude climate. So one must choose between the reddish mountain that the locals call the 'cathedral' near the village of Tilougguite and the natural amphitheater – the Cirque de Jaffar – which lies at the foot of Mt Abachi, the almost-Andean valley of Tizi n'Ouano and the arid Ait Youl, a mountain chain frequented by the itinerant Ait Atta population during its summer transhumance. The shepherds take their goats and sheep to mountain pastures and then make the return trip in mid-October, when it becomes cold and it is best to go back to the more hospitable southernmost slopes of Mt Saghro, to a sort pastoral republic based on an intricate mélange of nobility, authority, decency and tradition.

Because while time may be precious, good weather is indispensable. This is the case with the last *imdyazn*, the itinerant bards and musicians who in the hot months move from one village to another, becoming chroniclers, witnesses and moralists. And it is true for those who attempt the climb up the giant of the Atlas Mountains, Mt Toubkal, 13,675 ft (4168 m) high, which looms over the village of Imlil, almost as if to discourage the mountaineers and their guides who want to imitate the Marquis de Segonzac, who in 1923 succeeded in conquering the summit of this giant together with other mountaineers and were able to enjoy the breathtaking panoramic view of the Marrakech region and the cone of massive Mt Siroua.

Excursions. Such as the one movie director Martin Scorsese made in this land to shoot *Kundun*, the film about the Dalai Lama that came out in 1997, leaving money invested intelligently in initiatives that are useful to the rural community. Then there is the trip to Kelaa M'Goun, the Valley of Roses, with the light hues of the roses that bloom in spring, when heaps of petals and

FLYING HIGH MOROCCO

A village lies along a seasonal river in the Middle Atlas. Beyond the river are cultivated plots of land, a well-irrigated green area that descends from the mountains.

buds are bunched in the courtyards and left to dry and the local communities begin complex bargaining so that their raw material can be converted into ointments, perfumes, soap and aromas for sweets.

Farther south is the Anti-Atlas, yet another mountain range that has the rugged and arid aspect of the nearby Sahara platform. Here the weather regulates the rhythm of life, establishes the rules, and orients humans in their periodic moves. In autumn it drives thousands of Berbers toward the grandiose wasteland of Imilchil, over 6560 ft (2000 m) above sea level, to listen to the sweet and sad legend of two young people from different rival clans of the Ait Haddidou tribe who were in love and had to meet secretly because of the hostility of their families. One day they left their respective homes, walking through the pastures that mark the High and Middle Atlas Mts., where they cried so woefully that they filled two valleys with their tears, thus creating the so-called Isli and Tislit lakes, before letting themselves die of hunger and prostration. Every year, a *moussem*, a major holiday, allows the young people who live in these plateaus to meet and choose their partners, even though the intrusiveness of tourists has attenuated somewhat the spontaneity of this huge Berber pilgrimage to the tomb of a venerated *marabut* a few steps from a large livestock market. Because besides the folklore, a *moussem* is a break in time, a tribute to someone or something: a saint, clan chief, or sentiment. As author Tahar Ben Jelloun wrote, "[...] it is a stop on the way marked out by the desire of the soul." On the last day, dozens of adolescents holding hands under the watchful gaze of their relatives formally state their intention to get married. A fine example of the alchemy of the mountain Berbers: love has been used to explain the geography of the Atlas Mountains, as have the sentiments of two tender adolescents, in order to soften their rugged profile.

FLYING HIGH MOROCCO

359
The alignment of the crests of the High Atlas constitute a barrier between the most fertile part of Morocco, influenced by the Mediterranean, and the most arid sector, which penetrates the Sahara dunes.

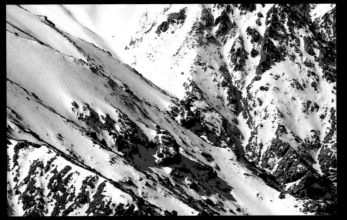

360
During the cold season it is possible to organize excursions into the Atlas Mts with mules and sports equipment.

361
The lower boundary of the snow line is rarely below 8200 ft (2500 m) on the north slope of the High Atlas and 9842 ft (3000 m) on the southern one. There is no permanent snow on the Atlas, but the peaks in the central Moroccan ranges are always covered with snow in the winter.

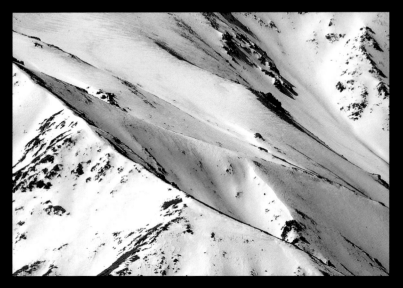

362
There are no perennial glaciers on the Atlas Mts., but the peaks in central Morocco are always snow-covered.

363
The High Atlas has attracted mostly mountaineers, but in recent years this chain has also been used for skiing and other winter sports.

365
Houses, vegetation, life: the High Atlas of the Berbers seems to be hospitable in this aerial view. This is due to the miracle of water, which flows down from the high-altitude snowfields and makes this region so fertile.

FLYING HIGH MOROCCO

366
The High Atlas consists of mountains that in general have little vegetation, valleys dotted with warren-like villages, and very rare communication routes.

368-369
The torrents that descend from the High Atlas sculpt the terrain, leaving huge traces of their passage and marking the habitat of the Berber communities.

371

Rainfall is heavier in the areas nearer to the Mediterranean and decreases drastically on the southernmost mountain ranges, that is, in the Middle and High Atlas.

372
In the early 1980s the Morocco Government launched pilot projects aimed at improving the rural economy in the Berber regions of the High Atlas.

373
In the High Atlas the houses are made of compressed mud, stones and straw.

FLYING HIGH MOROCCO

374
The Atlas villages once lived off livestock and the poorest form of agriculture, but can now supplement their income thanks to tourism: in these areas that used to be desolate, it is now easy to find lodgings with the Berber families.

376
At high altitudes the landscape of the High Atlas is like an arid steppe.

377
They are called 'gates,' but are really small rural hamlets that frame the High Atlas mountain range.

378 and 379

As is the case with many other rural civilizations, in the Atlas region the small farms look like human outposts facing the void. The presence of dry stone walls shows that in the recent past sheep raising was common in this region, but now it seems that the shepherds have moved off to the cities.

380
An interminable series of passes, narrow valleys, peaks and slopes with wavy color patterns: this is the magic of the High Atlas.

381
This barren and rolling terrain heralds the high plateaus around Imilchil.

382-383
The small settlements of the High Atlas are grouped in larger territorial units, in a complex hierarchical system of districts, provinces and regions.

FLYING HIGH MOROCCO

384
Together with the Rif, the High Atlas is the Moroccan region that has been influenced least by the economic growth the country is enjoying.

386
In the Mt M'Goun and Mt Toubkal area, finding a village offering lodging takes days of hard hiking.

387
The High Atlas is a paradise for trekking as well as photography buffs. In this part of Morocco, ancient geological phenomena have shaped the land, creating incredible scenery.

388
This plain close to the Atlas range, like so many others, is the object of arboriculture and planting projects. Investing ideas and funds in mountain agriculture is a possible solution to the abandonment of the rural areas now in progress.

389
In the more accessible areas of the High Atlas the population tends to groups together in small villages.

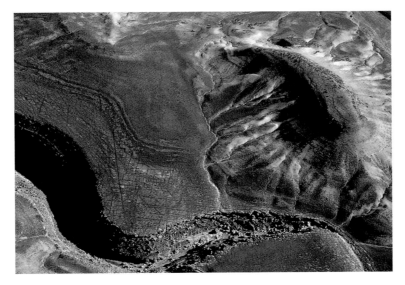

390 and 391

These highly imaginative abstract figures are really torrents without any life and absolutely barren terrain viewed from an airplane. This is the harsh environment in which the Berber communities of the High Atlas are forced to live.

392-393
A rugged mountainous region is the backdrop of the large urban area of Marrakech.

394

The Oude Dades River, which runs along the valley, has fed many oases. In fact, the valley is also known as the Valley of the Thousand Kasbahs.

395

Coppices and spontaneous vegetation can be seen along the slopes of the High Atlas Mountains, where the altitude favors rainfall, and the hills are transformed into cultivated land that closer one gets to Marrakech.

396
The green areas show that we are at the end of the High Atlas and are
approaching the Marrakech plain.

397
The road from Marrakech to Tizi-N'Tichkat is lined with the first Berber
villages in the High Atlas region.

398
The Ziz River winds its way among the easternmost High Atlas mountains.

399
The green belt of the Ziz River near Tinerhir is the gateway to the Tafilalt region.

400
The Hassan-Addakhil Dam was named after the first Alawite prince, who went to Tafilalt in the thirteenth century.

401
Built in 1971, Hassan-Addakhil 'Barrage' is a reservoir containing 470 million cu. yards (360 million cu. m) of water used for irrigation.

402-403
The huge Hassan-Addakhil reservoir contrasts sharply with the arid scenery of the Ziz River valley.

404-405
Desolate, and in certain points downright ghostly, the Dades River valley, situated south of Boulemane, has become a sort of Hollywood in the desert, as many movie directors have used it as a location for epic films.

406

Following the course of the river one sees less and less vegetation and more open spaces. But this is the magic of the Dades River valley: pure air and light that is already Saharan.

407

In the eternal cycle of dry and rainy seasons, the Dades River plows through arid and rough terrain before arriving at the oases that herald the desert.

408-409
An oasis that is an entrance to the Dades River Valley not far from Tamnalt.

410
There is enough rainfall in the Middle Atlas to give rise to small, verdant valleys along the course of the seasonal torrents.

411
The Dades River carves deep canyons in the south side of the High Atlas.

412

The Todra area is becoming a favorite with climbers. On the walls of the gorges there are interesting climbs of different categories of difficulty.

413

A difficult track goes beyond the Todra Gorges and reaches the Dades River valley via the Tizi n'Uguent Zegsaoun Pass, at an altitude of 8658 ft (2639 m).

414

The Oued Ziz River starts off in the Imilchil region and continues to the Algerian frontier, after having crossed over the fascinating Tafilalt zone, where one frequently comes upon the remains of *ksar*, the fortified villages along the old trade routes.

415

Citadels and *ksar*: the scenery along the Ziz River valley is among the most photogenic in southern Morocco.

416
The banks of the river that cuts through the Tafilalt region are dotted with small villages that are often uninhabited.

417
The road from Er Rachidia to Erfoud continually follows the course of the Ziz River, the only green patch in a region that is virtually a desert.

418

Kasbahs and Berber citadels lie on the shores of the Draa River, creating one of the postcard images of Morocco.

419

The last ridges of the High Atlas and Anti-Atlas end in the Draa River Valley, which is a sort of transition zone leading to the Sahara Desert.

420-421

For a stretch of several miles there are many towns along the road in the Draa River valley, some of which have preserved their age-old, high-quality handicrafts tradition.

422-423

Since ancient times, the verdant strip of the Draa River has been the site of true fortresses constructed to defend the population from marauders – kasbahs and *ksar*, which are fortified villages and castles made of straw and mud that blend in perfectly with the environment. Today many travel agencies offer non-invasive tours of these marvelous sites by means of long, fascinating treks on dromedaries.

424
The Draa River valley is a classical tourist attraction, but the architecture of the city and the oases is fortunately still preserved.

425
The ruins of an abandoned fortified city lie on a rise near one of the oases that skirt the Draa River.

426
Multi-layer ridges are typical of the areas that range from the Jebel Ougnat to the stony desert of Alnif and Mecissi.

427
The boundless region that goes from the Dades River valley to the Sahara Desert is enclosed on either side by the Tafilalt and Draa River valleys.

Index

Index

Index

PAOLO GALLIANI, WAS BORN IN DESIO (MILAN) IN 1952. HE IS A JOURNALIST AND SUBEDITOR OF THE DAILY NEWS DESK FOR THE DAILY NEWSPAPER *IL GIORNO.* A PASSIONATE TRAVELER AND AUTHOR OF NUMEROUS ARTICLES, FOR YEARS GALLIANI HAS WORKED IN THE FIELD OF FOREIGN POLICY AND HAS MADE GEOGRAPHIC DOCUMENTARIES FOR THE SWISS-ITALIAN TELEVISION ON BURMA, PERU, AND BOLIVIA. GALLIANI HAS ALSO WRITTEN SPECIALIZED GUIDEBOOKS; IN ADDITION, HE HAS BEEN INTERESTED IN MOROCCO FOR YEARS, ESPECIALLY ITS CULTURAL HERITAGE AND THE STUDY OF THE GEOGRAPHIC AND ANTHROPOLOGICAL ASPECTS OF THE COUNTRY.

Photo credits

All photographs are by Antonio Attini/Archivio White Star except the following:

pages 4-5 Gianni and Tiziana Baldizzone/Archivio White Star
page 9 Yann Arthus-Bertrand/Corbis
pages 38, 76-77, 80-81 Gianni and Tiziana Baldizzone/Archivio White Star
page 194 Yann Arthus-Bertrand/Corbis
page 196 Bruno Barbey/Magnum Photos/Contrasto
pages 197, 198 Yann Arthus-Bertrand/Corbis
page 201 Cécile Treal & Jean-Michel Ruiz/Hoa-Qui/HachettePhotos/Contrasto
pages 202, 203, 205, 206, 207 Yann Arthus-Bertrand/Corbis
page 209 Photononstop/Tips Images
pages 219, 240 Yann Arthus-Bertrand/Corbis
page 261 Fridmar Damm/zefa/Corbis
pages 264, 265 Yann Arthus-Bertrand/Corbis

The publisher would like to thank the pilot, Fiore Ambrogio and the Aero Club de Reus.

© 2008 WHITE STAR S.P.A.
Via Candido Sassone, 22-24
13100 Vercelli - Italy
WWW.WHITESTAR.IT

TRANSLATION: MADDALENA NEALE

ISBN 978-88-544-0342-0

REPRINTS: 1 2 3 4 5 6   12 11 10 09 08

Color separation: Chiaroscuro and Fotomec, Turin
Printed in China

432

The old town and the wall, with
the so-called Bastion dominating
the cliff, are the most precious
jewels of Asilah.

FLYING HIGH